Defending
Traditional
Marriage

Other books by Willard F. Harley, Jr.

Defending Traditional Marriage

![It Starts with You]

It Starts with You

WILLARD F. HARLEY, JR.

Revell

Grand Rapids, Michigan

Published by Fleming H. Revell
a division of Baker Publishing Group
P.O. Box 6287, Grand Rapids, MI 49516-6287

Printed in the United States of America

Library of Congress Cataloging-in-Publication Data
Harley, Willard F.
   Defending traditional marriage : it starts with you / Willard F. Harley, Jr.
      p.   cm.
   Includes bibliographical references and index.
   ISBN 0-8007-3109-3 (pbk.)
   1. Marriage—Religious aspects—Christianity. 2. Marriage. I. Title.
BV835.H365 2005
261.8′3581—dc22   2005014194

Contents

1 What's the Fuss All About?   7
   The Meaning of Traditional Marriage

Part 1 "To Love and to Cherish" ~ Extraordinary Care

2 What's Marriage without Love?   21
   The Love Bank

3 How to Make Each Other Happy   31
   Intimate Emotional Needs

4 How to Avoid Making Each Other Unhappy   51
   Love Busters

5 How to Create a Mutually Enjoyable Lifestyle   69
   The Policy of Joint Agreement

6 Our Culture and Care Don't Mix   91
   Overcoming Cultural Obstacles to Extraordinary Care

Part 2 **"Forsaking All Others" ~ Romantic Exclusivity**

7 One of Life's Most Devastating
Experiences 109
The Curse of Infidelity

8 The Law Is Wrong 121
Laws That Encourage Infidelity

9 How to Affair-Proof Your Marriage 143
*Overcoming Cultural and Legal Obstacles to
Romantic Exclusivity*

Part 3 **"Till Death Do Us Part" ~ Permanence**

10 When Is It Time to Call It Quits? 165
Divorce and Its Dire Consequences

11 Is "No-Fault" at Fault? 175
Laws That Encourage Divorce

12 How to Divorce-Proof Your Marriage 191
*Overcoming Cultural and Legal Obstacles to
Permanence*

Part 4 **"To Be Your Husband (or Wife)" ~ One Man,
One Woman**

13 Same-Sex Marriage a Threat? 209
*Is There Anything Wrong with Gay and Lesbian
Relationships?*

14 Is a Constitutional Amendment Really
Necessary? 219
The Defense of Marriage Act

15 Restoring the Meaning of Traditional
Marriage 231
*How the Same-Sex Marriage Issue Has Helped
Raise Public Awareness*

Notes 243
Index 248

1

What's the Fuss All About?

The Meaning of Traditional Marriage

It was Friday morning and I'd just finished breakfast when the telephone rang. Tom Prichard, president of the Minnesota Family Counsel, was asking me to testify that morning before the Minnesota Senate Judiciary Committee. As a clinical psychologist, I am sometimes called upon (on short notice!) by various organizations to defend or oppose pending legislation that might affect mental health. So when Tom's request came in, I cleared my schedule and went right to work on a presentation.

This time the issue was the definition of marriage. The pending legislation in this case, a proposed amendment to the state constitution, would limit marriage to one man and one woman. In doing so, it would deny eligibility for marriage to people in same-sex and polygamous relationships.

I realized this was a controversial issue. But as I was presenting my testimony, I never dreamed that it was so divisive it would end up deadlocking the Minnesota Senate. The Senate eventually adjourned without having addressed a host of other important bills just because they didn't want this issue brought to the floor for debate. By doing so, they prevented passage of a bill that would leave the definition of marriage in the hands of the people.

Minnesota isn't alone in wrestling with how to define marriage. The same debate is raging all over America. And extreme passion is driving both sides of the issue.

Why? What makes people care so much about this issue of defining marriage? It's the implications that come along with a definition of marriage that create such a stir. These implications are actually much broader than the one I addressed that Friday morning—whether or not marriage should be between one man and one woman—and have great significance for the future of traditional marriage itself.

In this book we'll talk about the many issues surrounding this great marriage debate. And you'll soon understand why some people are getting so fired up—on both sides of the issue. I'll also help you understand why this issue will be settled one way or another in the next few years and how that outcome will affect the future of your children.

Of course, none of this is new. Traditional marriage has been under attack in America for at least the past seventy years. And that attack has been successful in destroying many traditional marriages. About half now end in divorce, and half of those that remain intact are characterized by resignation or even misery rather than love and affection. Is it any wonder that couples are afraid to marry these days?

The Latest Wave

Court decisions giving those in the gay and lesbian communities the same right to marry as those in the heterosexual community are only the latest in a series of attacks on traditional marriage. We'll get to the earlier attacks in a moment, but for now let's consider the current battle under way.

Gays and lesbians argue that restricting marriage to a man and a woman is discrimination against them. So they view that restriction as a civil rights issue. Just as African-Americans were once relegated to the backs of buses because of their race, gays and lesbians argue that they are relegated to nonmarital unions because of their sexual orientation. What they want is to redefine marriage to include their preferred lifestyle.

There have been rumblings in the polygamy camp as well. They also try to make it a civil rights issue by arguing that none of us are wired for a single, lifelong relationship. After all, look at all the affairs that plague marriages these days.

At a time when so many marriages are filled with problems (consider the statistics I mentioned earlier), why are gays and lesbians so anxious to secure marital rights for themselves? Because, even with all its problems, marriage still offers many advantages over other relationships. Two of the most important advantages for married couples are stability and safety.

Historically, gay and lesbian relationships have tended to be rather brief, violent, and unhealthy. Because of rampant promiscuity, the spread of venereal and other diseases has resulted in notoriously short life spans. The same can be said of *heterosexual* couples who live together outside of marriage. Those relationships also tend to be brief, violent, and unhealthy—particularly when compared to relationships between married couples. So it's reasonable for gays and lesbians to identify marriage as one way to create stability and safety for their relationships.

There are also economic reasons cited—health care coverage and laws governing inheritance, for example. With mainstream acceptance of the "alternative" lifestyles, gays and lesbians increasingly want all the same privileges afforded heterosexual individuals in America.

So when the Massachusetts Supreme Court decided to grant marriage for gays and lesbians, proponents of such equality were quite optimistic. But along with the ruling came a firestorm of protest from those who see it as a threat to heterosexual marriage. Since that decision was made, the issue has created so much heat that it may remain near the top of the list of political issues for some time to come.

Why are heterosexual married couples getting so upset about something that may help gay and lesbian relationships? Why not share their safety and security with those who do not share their sexual orientation? The reason is that many advocates of traditional marriage see gay and lesbian marriage as a huge threat to the institution of marriage itself—and they're right.

But I also see the same-sex marriage debate as an unprecedented opportunity to draw attention to the relentless decline of traditional marriage in America and other parts of the Western world—and to stop that decline. If the issue of same-sex marriage forces us to look at marriage as something worth defining—and saving—I couldn't be happier that it has come to our attention.

A Disaster in the Making

Over the past seventy-five years, the meaning of marriage in America has been changing so slowly that few have been aware of the change. So it takes a little work to uncover the traditional meaning of marriage. Let's start by considering the wedding vow itself.

A minister usually asks the groom some variation of the following question: "Will you take this woman to be your wife, to live together in the covenant of marriage? Will you love her, comfort her, honor and keep her, in joy and in sorrow, in plenty and in want, in sickness and in health, and, forsaking all others, be faithful to her so long as you both shall live?"

If the groom makes this promise, the minister asks the same question of the bride: "Will you take this man to be your husband, to live together in the covenant of marriage? Will you love him, comfort him, honor and keep him, in joy and in sorrow, in plenty and in want, in sickness and in health, and, forsaking all others, be faithful to him so long as you both shall live?"

When the bride agrees, the minister announces that, based on the promises the couple have made to each other, he can pronounce them husband and wife. So it's reasonable to assume that these vows describe what it means to be married in the traditional sense. A closer look reveals qualities that may be expressed in the following definition:

> **Traditional marriage** *is a permanent (as long as you both shall live) and sexually exclusive (forsaking all others) relationship of extraordinary care (love, comfort, honor, and keep, etc.) between a man (to be your husband) and a woman (to be your wife).*

This is what almost every marriage vow has declared down through the ages. For thousands of years couples have known that these are all essential for a successful marriage. By definition, then, a traditional marriage is (1) permanent, (2) sexually exclusive, (3) characterized by extraordinary care, and (4) between a man and a woman.

A Greater Purpose

This definition of traditional marriage drawn from common wedding vows provides a pretty clear picture of marital expectations. But what it doesn't show is the primary goal of traditional marriage—to raise the offspring of the husband and wife in an environment of safety and security. Wedding vows don't explicitly state that objective, but each of the four parts of the vow itself assists couples in becoming successful parents to the children they help create.

In all honesty, when I married my wife, Joyce, I wasn't thinking about children at all. I assumed we would raise children, but I didn't marry her with that goal in mind. I married her because I was in love with her, and I wanted us to share our lives with each other.

Yet looking back on forty-two years of a very romantic and happy marriage with Joyce, I can see clearly that, apart from our relationship with God, our children *have* been the most important result of our marriage. And by keeping our wedding vows, we've helped make our children happy and successful. I also realize now that if our children had turned out to be unhappy and had been failures in life, Joyce and I would have been miserable despite our love for each other and an otherwise great life together.

That's the way most couples feel about their offspring. They want their children to have every advantage in life. And the greatest advantage of all is being raised by parents

12

whose marriage is permanent, sexually exclusive, and characterized by extraordinary care for each other.

Granted, there are other important reasons to marry. Most people, like Joyce and me, marry because they're in love, and they want to spend their lives together. Even if a couple doesn't have any children to raise, or if they raise children who are not genetically related to both of them, marriage has so many important advantages over nonmarital relationships that it's certainly well worth having. But as important as those other advantages are, they can't compare to the advantage that traditional marriage gives children.

So as traditional marriage has been under attack, children have been the primary victims. When the divorce rate climbed from 10 percent to 50 percent in the 1960s and '70s, many argued that the children of divorce would be just fine. Some even argued that they would turn out better than children raised in traditional families. But now the results are in.

The attack on traditional marriage has had a devastating effect on children. There are many ways to measure this tragedy, but one of the most impressive is crime. Our prisons are bulging at the seams with men and women who have not been raised in traditional families. And their population grows by the minute. By contrast, the number of those in prison today who were raised in a traditional family is much smaller.[1]

Consider the cost of educating children raised in traditional families compared to the cost of educating those raised without their biological mother and father. Anyone with any experience teaching will agree that the difference is staggering. And has all of the added expense helped? So far we've found that no amount of money for special programs can compensate for the value of being raised in a traditional family. We will probably spend billions of dollars in the future to try to compensate for the value of lost traditional families, and not one dime of it will help. The Federal "No Child Left Behind" program ignores the fact that the children left behind are those not raised by their biological parents. It's not the schools that have left them behind—it's their parents.

On average, those who grew up without the benefits of a traditional family earn less, produce less, are less educated, are not as healthy, and are not as happy as those who were raised in traditional families.[2] Seeing these results, many social scientists have changed their tune. They are now beginning to recognize the value of traditional families and are trying to save them. But is it too late? Have we gone too far in destroying the values that made traditional families thrive?

In this book I'll describe how our culture, state legislatures, and the courts no longer support the type of marriage that provides children with the safety and security they need. I'll show how they've eliminated the permanence of marriage by creating laws that encourage divorce. And I'll explain how they've undermined the sexual exclusivity of marriage by creating laws that encourage infidelity.

With the values of permanence and sexual exclusivity removed, the battle is now raging over why we should keep marriage between just a man and a woman. Marriage is slowly turning into little more than a temporary and promiscuous relationship between any two (or more in some cases) people—and children are the ultimate victims of this "evolution."

Four Essential Ingredients

I've divided this book into four parts, each focusing attention on one of the four basic elements of traditional marriage. Although the catalyst for this discussion is the issue of same-sex marriage, I'll save that subject for last.

Part 1: Extraordinary Care

In their wedding vows a couple promise to "love, comfort, honor, and keep" each other in any of life's circumstances: "in joy and in sorrow, in plenty and in want, in sickness and in health." Couples making this promise don't intend to care for each other only when times are good. They promise to care for each other when times are bad as well. And if, at the time of the wedding, one of them refused to make that promise, few would be willing to go through with the ceremony.

I've spent my entire professional career teaching couples how to provide that kind of care for each other because it's absolutely essential in creating a happy marriage. It's also essential in creating an environment for children who will grow up to become happy and successful. So in this first section of the book, I'll describe the three aspects of extraordinary care and explain how they lead to a happy marriage. I'll also explain how our me-first culture discourages extraordinary care in marriage and how you can provide that care despite what society teaches.

Part 2: Sexual Exclusivity

When a couple marry, they promise to "forsake all others" and be "faithful" to each other—sexually. Faithfulness in marriage is so fundamental to the marriage agreement that when the vow is broken, most marriages go into a freefall. Infidelity ranks as one of the most painful experiences of a betrayed spouse's life. Anyone who knew at the time of their wedding that their spouse would eventually have an affair would refuse to marry that person. It's that important to remain faithful.

But affairs do not harm just marriages—they also harm children. A child also feels betrayed by a parent who cheats and then lies about it. Can you think of a worse example to a developing child than an unfaithful father or mother?

Yet our laws encourage infidelity in marriage. Instead of protecting marriage from interlopers, the law protects the interloper. And because there are no laws against it, affairs have increased to such an extent that the majority of marriages now fall victim. Part 2 of this book will give you an overview of how this has happened and what can be done to change it. It will also show you how to protect your own marriage from the threat of infidelity in spite of laws and cultural values that encourage it.

Part 3: Permanence

A couple who marry promise to remain together "as long as we both shall live," and that promise is essential to marriage for a host of reasons. The most important reason is that stability and continuity are required for raising children successfully. If a couple were told on the day of their wedding that they would divorce when their children were young and needed them the most, they would stop the ceremony. Even if a couple knew they could only avoid divorce until their children became adults, I'm not sure they would agree to be married. That's because marriage creates interdependence—both spouses come to need each other in order to thrive. A divorce at any stage of life rips them apart, damaging both of them.

The relentless attack on traditional marriage that began in the 1930s started to affect the divorce rate in the 1960s and '70s. The cultural emphasis on self-centeredness during those decades caused couples to file for divorce in unprecedented numbers. But instead of passing laws to encourage couples to care for each other and restore their marriage, laws were passed making divorce easier than it had ever been. An unhappy spouse no longer needed a reason to break a commitment that had profound implications to children and to society. Instead it could be broken without justification.

In part 3 of this book, I'll show you how no-fault divorce laws were enacted and the effect they've had on traditional marriage. I'll also explain what you can do to avoid divorce despite the current laws and culture that encourage it.

Part 4: One Man and One Woman

In part 4 we'll focus our attention on the most important reason for limiting marriage to one man and one woman—the fact that it's the best way to raise happy and successful children. No one can replace a father and a mother united in marriage who love their children and love each other.

Since gay and lesbian marriages have only been legal in some countries for the past few years, we don't have much information about how well they actually work out in practice. And we have even less information about how well children turn out when raised by a same-sex couple. But we do know that children tend to do very well in a traditional family. In the 1960s and '70s we were told that children would do just fine after their parents divorced. But the experiment failed, and millions of children were the victims. Why experiment with the future of children when we already know what works?

Throughout this book, I'll challenge you to understand the importance of your wedding vows and to take them seriously in spite of the fact that our laws and culture do not. I'll also challenge you to do your part to try to change existing laws that threaten traditional marriage for the sake of future generations of children.

I know these seem like pretty lofty goals. But I'm convinced that we now have an unprecedented opportunity to defend traditional marriage and its value to children and to society itself—an opportunity we can't afford to miss. It all starts with you.

PART I

"TO LOVE AND TO CHERISH"

Extraordinary Care

2

What's Marriage without Love?

The Love Bank

When Joyce and I were married, I assumed that I'd be in love with her for the rest of my life. But I knew that I'd care for her regardless of my feelings. That's because I had promised to cherish her—to provide extraordinary care. It didn't matter how I felt or what kind of circumstances came our way. I would never stop caring for her, and we would always be together.

So when I began my career as a marriage counselor, I was shocked when couples calmly explained to me that they intended to divorce because they were *no longer in love*. These couples reported that their passion for each other had died, giving way to feelings of apathy, and, in some cases, even hatred. Because their feelings had changed, they did not want to care for each other.

How could that be? I wondered. *They had promised to love and cherish each other for life. Didn't their promises mean anything to them?*

For me, divorce was simply not an option. I made a vow to care for Joyce "till death do us part," and I considered myself bound by that vow. I planned to love and cherish Joyce for life, and I expected her to do the same for me. But the couples I was counseling didn't share my commitment. I was witnessing the start of a major culture shift, and it was having a profound impact on people's attitudes toward love and marriage.

It was the midsixties when I first started counseling, and a revolution was taking place in society. I had been raised to consider the interests of others before my own, but the couples I was counseling were part of a new generation that was raised to take care of *themselves* first. Other-centeredness had shifted to self-centeredness, and that shift was having a devastating effect on marriage—and on the feeling of love.

In case after case, divorcing spouses told me they had cared for their spouse too long—it was now time to take care of themselves. In most cases, though, there was little evidence that they'd ever shown much care for their spouse. In reality, they'd spent most of their married lives caring for themselves at their spouse's expense. After a few years of mutual selfishness, it was no wonder they wanted a divorce.

Self-help books tended to support selfishness as an ideal. "Experts" at colleges and universities all over America encouraged people, especially women, to look out for themselves in marriage. Many even argued that marriage was a terribly outdated trap for most women—a source of enslavement and misery. In book after book, women were portrayed as care*givers* and men as care*takers*. As a result, women initiated three out of four divorces at that time.

22

When I tried to convince couples that divorce was ultimately self-destructive, not to mention harmful to their children, most didn't believe me. They didn't think their decision would hurt anyone, least of all themselves. People accused me of trying to make divorcing spouses feel guilty for something that was their right—the freedom to make whatever decisions suited their own best interests.

Unfortunately for those who didn't believe me, research was clearly on my side. Divorced couples really did tend to be unhappy about it years later, and the children of divorced parents grew up to be less happy and less successful than the children of those who remained married. But the facts and common sense were totally outweighed by the popular belief that every person should be free to do whatever he or she felt was right.

So I stopped trying to convince couples that divorce was a mistake. Since I was being told that the primary reason for divorce was the loss of love, I came to the conclusion that the best way to save marriages was to restore that love. If I could help couples recreate their love for each other, they would no longer want to divorce.

Most of my colleagues did not believe that the feeling of love was sustainable in marriage. They had observed that after as little as a few months—three years at most—a married couple would lose the passion they once had for each other. However, I had one piece of crucial evidence to the contrary—at that time I had been married for over ten years, and Joyce and I were still passionately in love. From personal experience, I knew it could be done.

My training as a behavioral psychologist also gave me an advantage over my pessimistic colleagues. They had been taught that people should accept themselves and others as they were and that they should avoid trying to change people. On the other hand, I had been taught that change in people is often desirable, and I had learned how to help people change their habits and their emotional reactions. So I was able to use my professional training and the experience of my own marriage to teach couples how to fall in love and stay in love.

So what was it that Joyce and I were doing that sustained our love for each other? And what had divorcing couples failed to do? It all boiled down to one crucial concept: extraordinary care.

Extraordinary Care—the Essential Ingredient

When I married Joyce, I planned to spend my life trying to figure out ways to make her happy and keep her feeling fulfilled. And I expected her to do the same for me. I didn't feel *pressured* to provide that quality of care—it was something I *wanted* to do. I looked forward to caring for her, and she let me know that she would enjoy caring for me, too.

But if at the time of our wedding Joyce had informed me that I shouldn't expect much care from her—little affection, conversation, sex, or even companionship—I would have been tempted to pull the plug on the ceremony. If she had gone on to warn me to expect plenty of fights, I'd have definitely told our guests that the wedding was on hold pending further discussion. And if she'd notified me that her ambitions would eventually leave me in the dust, our marriage would have been out of the question for me.

Joyce and I married because we loved each other. But the only reason we're still in love with each other today—forty-two years later—is that we've given each other the extraordinary care we both expected on the day of our wedding. If we had stopped caring for each other after our wedding vows had been spoken, it wouldn't have taken long before our love for each other would have vanished. And if our love had vanished, our very marriage would have been at risk, along with the happiness and success of our children. They desperately needed us to love each other, and that love required our extraordinary care.

I'll let you in on a simple fact that completely transformed my understanding of how to save marriages: **If spouses give each other the extraordinary care throughout life that they expect at the time of their wedding, they will never lose their love for each other.** Joyce and I, along with millions of other couples, are living examples of how that principle works.

Even if you haven't always lived that principle, it's never too late to start. I've taught thousands of couples how to restore lost love simply by starting to give each other the extraordinary care they should have been giving all along.

Romantic Love and the Love Bank

The feeling of love—I call it **romantic love**—is quite predictable. It's that predictability that makes me so successful in saving marriages. I know what creates romantic love, what destroys it, and what can sustain it for a lifetime. And I use that knowledge to help married couples recapture romantic love for each other even after they think it has been lost for good.

I want you to acquire that same knowledge so that your marriage can be as fulfilling for you and your spouse as my marriage has been for Joyce and me. To help you understand how romantic love works, I'll begin by introducing you to a concept I call the Love Bank.

There is a Love Bank inside each one of us. Our emotions use it to keep track of the way people treat us. Every person we've ever known has an account in our Love Bank, and their balances are determined by how we feel when we are with them. If someone makes us feel good, love units are deposited into their account. But if we feel bad around this person, love units are withdrawn. The better we feel, the more love units are deposited. The worse we feel, the more are withdrawn.

Our emotions make us feel attracted to or repulsed by a person based on the balance in his or her Love Bank account. When someone has a positive Love Bank balance—more deposits than withdrawals—our emotions cause us to *like* him or her. But when someone has a negative balance—more withdrawals than deposits—our emotions cause us to *dislike* that person.

The larger the positive balance in someone's Love Bank account, the more attracted we feel to that person. For example, if 200 love units accumulate, we feel pretty good about someone; if 500 love units accumulate, we may consider that person to be one of our best friends.

But something special happens when the Love Bank balance of someone of the opposite sex reaches a critical threshold of, say, 1,000 love units. Our emotions give us a special feeling that we call romantic love. When we have that feeling for someone, we want to spend as much time as possible with that person—even for the rest of our lives!

Of course, negative balances have the opposite effect. Just like a checking account, a Love Bank account can be in the red when love units continue to be withdrawn after none are left. If someone at work who has been annoying eventually has a Love Bank balance of negative 200, our emotions will make us feel uncomfortable whenever that person is around, even when he or she is not doing anything that's annoying. And someone with a Love Bank balance of negative 500 will seem downright repulsive. We will try to avoid that person whenever possible.

But when someone has a very large negative balance, say negative 1,000 love units, our emotions make that person seem particularly repulsive. We feel hatred toward that person, and go to great lengths to avoid *all* contact.

It happens automatically if a person's balance in our Love Bank dips to that critical low point.

We don't end up reaching that hate threshold with most people because we stop having contact with them before their Love Bank balance falls that far. But within marriage, it's a different story. Why? Because we can't easily avoid the relentless withdrawals of love units if our spouse is the one who is making us unhappy.

It's possible to escape from just about everyone else, thus putting an end to Love Bank withdrawals. If you work with a very rude and inconsiderate person, you can request another office and simply avoid contact as much as possible. Even in the case of a next-door neighbor, you can try to ignore that person or even move, if necessary.

But in marriage, escape isn't so easy. If you're not filling each other's Love Banks as a couple, you're probably emptying them. And if you empty them long enough, your emotions will scream, "Get out of here!" As you continue to make each other miserable, your Love Bank balance may eventually reach negative 1,000—the hate threshold—and you'll feel incredibly repulsed by your spouse whenever he or she is around. That's when divorce starts to seem the only reasonable way to escape what has become a living nightmare.

But divorce *isn't* the only way to escape the negative Love Bank cycle. It's true that our emotional reactions make it seem impossible to ever be in love again when Love Bank balances are negative. But it can be done. And as negative balances turn positive, our emotional reactions change as well. We eventually stop feeling repulsed and start feeling attracted instead.

If you're in love with each other today, it's because you've learned to make Love Bank deposits and avoid withdrawals. But if you dislike each other today, or even hate each other, you've forgotten how to give the extraordinary care you promised on your wedding day.

In spite of what the so-called experts have said, romantic love *doesn't* have to fade away with time. You and your spouse can be as in love today as you were the day you married—if you understand a second kind of love as well.

Caring Love

Romantic love is not the only kind of love. There's another kind of love that is also very important in marriage. I call it **caring love**—a willingness and effort to try to make someone happy and to try to avoid making that person unhappy. While romantic love is a feeling, caring love is a decision.

People can have caring love in many types of relationships. The love you have for your children is caring love. You may also care for your parents and close friends. In fact, you may care for people you don't even know when you decide to invest time and resources with charitable organizations that help those people. Caring love in marriage is expressed by your time and effort to make your spouse happy and improve his or her quality of life.

But as committed as you might be, you may not actually be building Love Bank balances with that effort. For example, a husband may show his care by purchasing jewelry for his wife. But what if his wife doesn't want jewelry? What if she craves some heart-to-heart conversation instead? If the husband is too busy to fill her need for conversation, his marriage will be headed for disaster, no matter how much jewelry he gives her.

Some marriage counselors think your spouse just wants to know you care. But they're wrong. Knowing that you care isn't enough to sustain romantic love. I've counseled hundreds of couples who care about each other but still have filed for divorce. Why? Because their care for each other has failed a crucial test—it doesn't deposit enough love units to break through the romantic love threshold. And the only way to achieve that crucial objective is to do more than just *try* to make your spouse happy and *try* to avoid making your spouse unhappy: you must *succeed.*

Caring love creates romantic love when your care for each other is effective—and extraordinary. If you give each other what you expected on your wedding day, your romantic love for each other will be sustained throughout life.

But there are forces at work that prevent you from giving each other the extraordinary care you need. Some of these forces are internal—we seem to be wired to stop giving each other what's needed in marriage and to start hurting each other. Other forces are external—we're part of a culture that encourages us to be thoughtless and uncaring and discourages us from providing the extraordinary care required for a terrific marriage.

You can resist those internal and external pressures if you know what they are and how to defend your marriage from their influence. In the next few chapters I'll show you how to give each other extraordinary care in marriage despite what popular opinion or cultural influences suggest. If you follow my advice, your Love Bank balances will be high enough to sustain your romantic love for each other indefinitely. And that's where a defense of traditional marriage must begin—with your love and care for each other.

3

How to Make Each Other Happy
Intimate Emotional Needs

During the first year of my marriage, I belonged to a chess club that met once a week. Every Wednesday evening I played chess with other club members while my wife, Joyce, sat at home alone watching television. It was a defining issue in our marriage. Joyce didn't want to learn to play chess with me, and she didn't want me to give up skills I'd spent years developing. Yet she felt lonely without me. Should she find something to do on Wednesday evening that would be just as enjoyable for her as chess was for me, or should I give up chess and switch to something we could do together?

Throughout our courtship we had taken every opportunity to be together. I would have never played chess with a bunch of old men if being with Joyce had been an option. Yet after we were married, it seemed reasonable. After all, we were now living together.

I didn't know it at the time, but that chess club could have prevented us from making each other happy. At the time it didn't seem that important because it was only one night a week, and we had plenty of time to make each other happy on other evenings. But after children arrived, and I was trying to finish school while supporting a family, I might have hung on to that chess club as my one opportunity to relax and get away from it all—without Joyce.

We missed each other so much on Wednesday nights that it didn't take long for me to abandon the chess club. Then two years later when time and money were tight and I needed to get away from it all to relax, Joyce was there relaxing with me. In spite of children and financial stress, Joyce and I had decided to spend our leisure time making each other happy. That's because we cared for each other—extraordinarily.

But making each other happy is only one part of extraordinary care. The other two are doing what you can to avoid hurting each other and creating a lifestyle that benefits both of you. When you provide this kind of care to each other, it's truly extraordinary, and it sustains your feeling of love throughout life.

All three parts of this extraordinary care are crucial in a marriage. If you're missing even *one* of them, romantic love won't survive and your marriage is at great risk of ending. But there is one of the three parts that does more to create romantic love than the other two combined: making each other happy. So let's start there.

It's just common sense really. How else could you deposit enough love units to break through the romantic love threshold in your spouse's Love Bank?

Making each other happy is the most obvious form of care in marriage. But because of common cultural beliefs and practices, it's not easy to do. Part of the problem is that many don't believe that we can, or should, try to make anyone else happy. Have you ever heard someone say, "You can't please everyone"? It seems that today most people believe that you can't really please *anyone* but yourself. They argue that true happiness comes from within, not from other people, and that each person should be responsible for his or her own happiness. This belief came into its own during the 1960s and '70s when we all were encouraged to take better care of *ourselves* and let others take care of *themselves*. Whenever I hear that point of view, I cringe because I know where it leads—to unapologetic selfish behavior. And in marriage, that kind of behavior generally leads to divorce.

Deep down we all know that we can make others happy—we've all done it. And we can also make others miserable if we're not careful. In other words, what we do *does* affect others, regardless of what anyone says to the contrary. In the language of the Love Bank, almost everything we do makes deposits or withdrawals. And the person who is most affected by what we do is the person we've chosen to marry.

That's why whenever I counsel a couple, I talk with each spouse separately about what he or she wants from the other. And it turns out that what they want most is the fulfillment of very basic emotional needs.

Emotional Needs

We all know about physical needs—food, water, oxygen, warmth, and so forth. These are essential to our survival. With them our bodies thrive. Without them, we die.

But we all have another kind of need as well—emotional needs. When these needs are not met, we don't die. For that reason, some people don't like to call them needs;

they prefer to call them *desires* or *wants*. But no matter what you call them, they can be just as compelling as physical needs. And in most cases, they are what motivate us to accomplish objectives that make our lives meaningful.

So to be sure we're on the same page, let me give you my definition: **An emotional need is a craving that, when satisfied, leaves us feeling happy and content, and when unsatisfied leaves us feeling unhappy and frustrated.**

There are thousands of emotional needs—a need for vacations, for fishing (for some men), for shopping (for most women). . . . I could go on and on, but you get the idea. Whenever one of our emotional needs is met, we feel good; when it's unmet, we feel bad. Try telling a football fan that he can't watch his favorite team play this week and you'll get a taste of how emotional needs affect people.

But not all emotional needs are created equal. Some of them make us feel comfortable when they're met—and they make small Love Bank deposits in doing so. There are others, however, that can make us feel downright euphoric when met. These make much larger Love Bank deposits. And when someone of the opposite sex meets *those* needs, it makes us so happy that we're likely to fall in love with the person. I call those needs our *most important emotional needs* because, when met, they make the largest Love Bank deposits of all.

Extraordinary Care Meets the Most Important Emotional Needs

When I finally decided that the best way to save marriages was by helping couples restore their feeling of love for each other, my first task was to figure out what would make the largest Love Bank deposits. So I went right to the source: I simply asked spouses to tell me what things made them the happiest when others did them and the most frustrated when they didn't.

How would you answer that question? Think for a minute about the last time your spouse did something for you that made you feel terrific. What happened to make you feel that way?

When I first started asking this question, I didn't know what the answers would be, and I didn't want to guess. But after asking hundreds of men and women, a pattern began to emerge. To my surprise, almost everyone gave answers that could be classified into one or more of a short list of categories: admiration, affection, conversation, domestic support, family commitment, financial support, honesty and openness, physical attractiveness, recreational companionship, and sexual fulfillment. I'm guessing that the situation you thought of for yourself probably fits into one of those categories as well because it seems that we're all wired similarly when it comes to the most important emotional needs.

Along with the discovery of this list of common emotional needs, I realized something else that helped me understand why husbands and wives might have trouble making each other happy. Whenever I asked spouses to prioritize these ten emotional needs, men tended to list them one way and women the opposite way. The five listed as most important by men were usually the five least important for women and vice versa.

On average, men told me that they needed sexual fulfillment and recreational companionship most, with physical attractiveness, domestic support, and admiration coming in third, fourth, and fifth on their lists. And on average, women told me that they needed affection and intimate conversation most, with honesty and openness, financial support, and family commitment making up their remaining top five needs. So in marriage the golden rule—do for your spouse what you would want your spouse to do for you—wouldn't work!

Intimate Emotional Needs

All ten of the emotional needs I identified are important in establishing healthy Love Bank balances, but there are four in particular that deposit so many love units that they tend to leave the others in the dust. These four can trigger romantic love so quickly that I focus most of my attention on training couples to meet these needs for each other first. I call those four needs the *intimate* emotional needs because I've found them to be met in almost all romantic relationships. For most men, they are sexual fulfillment and recreational companionship, and for most women, they are intimate conversation and affection.

When all four of those needs are met regularly in marriage, both the husband and wife are very happy—romantic love is almost guaranteed. But if only the husband's needs or only the wife's needs are met, it doesn't take long before romantic love disappears for the one whose needs are not being met. When that happens, that person loses the will to continue meeting the other spouse's needs, which means that the intimate emotional needs of both spouses end up being unmet.

So how can you be sure that you are meeting each of these intimate emotional needs in your marriage? Let's take a closer look.

Intimate Conversation

Conversation is the most common way to begin a relationship. And the most common way to begin a *romantic* relationship is with *intimate* conversation. If you talk with someone of the opposite sex about your deepest feelings and your most personal problems, you're engaged in the type of conversation that can bond you emotionally to that person. And since it can be so intense and enjoyable, it's easy to fall in love with that person.

Ordinary conversation is an emotional need that can be ethically met by anyone. But when conversation is intimate, with someone of the opposite sex, it's likely to lead to a romantic relationship. That's why I advise married couples to limit their intimate conversation to each other.

Romantic relationships thrive on intimate conversation. It helps create the relationship, and it helps sustain it. Without it, romantic relationships are simply not romantic.

Recreational Companionship

Recreational activities provide pure enjoyment; they give you something to look forward to after you complete all your responsibilities. That's why they're an extremely important part of a romantic relationship—they make Love Bank deposits seem almost effortless. When a man and woman are in a romantic relationship, they are almost always each other's favorite recreational companions.

Before you were married, you probably planned your dates around recreational activities. You wanted to be certain that you were both enjoying yourselves when you were together, so you chose activities that would make that possible. You may not have known it at the time, but if you hadn't spent your recreational time with each other, you probably wouldn't have created the romantic relationship that led to marriage.

The same thing is true once you're married. When your most enjoyable and relaxing time is spent apart from each other, you're no longer in a romantic relationship. Many couples have been led to believe that men need to participate in certain activities that women cannot enjoy and

Intimate Conversation's Friends and Enemies

THESE FOUR FRIENDS will help intimate conversation flourish between you and your spouse:

1. Understand each other: *Investigate* by asking each other personal questions such as, How are you feeling? What are you thinking? What have you been doing? What are you planning? What's been bothering you? *Inform* each other by answering those questions honestly whenever they're asked. Such deep and personal inquiry and revelation provides an intimate understanding of each other that would be difficult to achieve any other way.

2. Discuss each other's favorite topics: *Educate* yourselves in these topics to make your conversation interesting for both of you. You can either develop an understanding of topics that interest both of you, or you can ignore those topics. If you develop them, your conversation will be enjoyable. But if you ignore them, eventually you won't have much to say to each other.

3. Provide balance: Each of you should *talk and listen about the same amount of time.* Don't interrupt each other or talk so much that your spouse has no opportunity to say anything. And don't let your spouse do all the talking. Intimate conversation is mutual and bilateral. You should both be good listeners and good talkers.

4. Give each other undivided attention: *Look into each other's eyes* as you talk. Avoid

vice versa. So instead of discovering activities to enjoy together, they decide to part company and find like-minded friends. Eventually they find themselves looking forward to being separated because that's when they have the most fun. And if the recreational companion is someone of the opposite sex, it can be downright dangerous.

The solution is simple—don't engage in any recreational activities that you can't enjoy together until you've found those you do enjoy together. Then, when you've found those shared activities, think of all the love units you could distractions. If your eyes wander around the room while you're talking, it sends the message that something else is more important. But when you talk intimately, nothing should be more important to you than the conversation you're having with your spouse.

THESE FOUR ENEMIES will destroy intimacy and drive your spouse away:

1. Demands: Whenever you tell your spouse what to do, instead of making a request, conversation turns ugly. You're not a sergeant and your spouse isn't a private, so demands should never be part of your conversation.

2. Disrespectful judgments: If you think you can "straighten out" your spouse, or if you find humor in making fun of your spouse, think again. Intimacy makes people very vulnerable to disrespect, so be careful in the way you communicate your opinions of each other.

3. Angry outbursts: It goes without saying that an angry outburst in the midst of an intimate conversation is devastating. Don't use angry outbursts to make your point. No one wants to be intimate with an angry monster.

4. Dwelling on mistakes: Mistakes must be addressed somehow, but it's *dwelling* on them that ruins intimate conversation. You may be thinking quite a bit about your spouse's past mistakes, but if you talk about them as much as you're thinking about them, eventually you'll be talking to yourself.

be depositing in the Love Bank of the one you should love the most—your spouse. That's why I encourage you to be each other's favorite recreational companions. With a little trial and error, you'll discover mutually enjoyable activities that have been there all along. And it's one of the simplest ways to make large Love Bank deposits.

Affection

When we care for someone, we express that care through affection. A hug sends the message, "You're important to me, and I'm concerned about problems you face. I'll help you overcome them." Hugs that are given to friends, relatives, children, and even pets, can communicate a simple message of your willingness to care.

But affection in marriage goes much farther. It communicates the willingness to provide the extraordinary care expected in a romantic relationship. In other words, affection is the way we let our spouse know that we care enough to do everything that makes a marriage work. It's the symbolic reminder that we will always provide extraordinary care.

Studies have shown that one of the quickest ways to make someone fall in love with you is to say you care for that person and then prove it by the way you treat him or her over the following days. That's because affection meets a very important emotional need, especially in women. It lets them know that much more is in store for them in the future if they give you a chance to prove your willingness and ability to care for them. With affection, you make Love Bank deposits by simply promising future care.

You may express affection in many ways: a greeting card or an "I love you" note, a bouquet of flowers, hugs, holding hands, walks after dinner, back rubs, phone calls, and conversations with thoughtful and loving expressions all can communicate affection. Of course, if the promised care is not forthcoming in the weeks, months, and years of the relationship, then all the hugs and kisses become meaningless and downright irritating. But if affection is backed up by the care you are already providing, those hugs deposit carloads of love units each time they're given.

While almost everyone has a need for affection, you've probably noticed that a husband's need is not usually as intense as the wife's need. Husbands like to be told they are loved, but they don't generally have the craving for affection that their wives have. That's why I encourage

Profile of an Affectionate Husband

An affectionate husband hugs and kisses his wife every morning while still in bed, usually for more than five minutes, and tells her that he loves her. During their breakfast, he tells her again that he loves her. I le hugs and kisses her before he leaves for work. He calls her during the morning and again in the afternoon to ask how she is doing and to tell her that he loves her. Sometimes he invites her to go out for lunch, and sometimes they both meet at home for lunch so he can hug and kiss her and tell her that he loves her. After work, he calls before he leaves for home, so that she knows when to expect him. When he arrives home, he gives her a hug and kiss and spends a few minutes talking with her about her day. He helps her with dinner and helps her clean up afterwards. He spends the evening with her, occasionally dancing to romantic music or giving her a back rub. When they go to bed, he usually hugs and kisses her while telling her that he loves her.

Does that description sound unreal? Well, I didn't come up with it by myself. It comes from scores of women who told me what they want most from their husbands. And it also describes what goes on during a typical romantic relationship—it's what men tend to do when they are in love.

every husband to create an *environment of affection* with his wife by making it a way of life.

If you have a need for affection, make a list of the expressions of affection that mean the most to you so that your spouse will know how to meet your need. I realize that affection should come from the heart, and giving your spouse a list of affectionate behavior may seem contrived. But take my word for it: if you have a need for affection, you'll like what he or she does, even if it seems a little awkward at first. And once your spouse gets into the habit of meeting your need for affection, it *will* be heartfelt and creative.

It takes repetition to form a habit. The more you practice a behavior, the easier it is to perform. But there's also

Who Starts It?

Couples frequently ask me who should take the initiative when it comes to affection. My answer is very important because it clears up a crucial misunderstanding that often leads to deep resentment.

When a wife complains to her husband that he isn't being affectionate enough, he makes a serious mistake when he advises her, "If you want a hug, come on over and hug me." His suggestion misses the point. She doesn't just need a hug, she needs assurance that he cares for her. She needs him to hug her as an expression of his care. To expect her to initiate affection is like telling his wife to pick out his Valentine's Day card for her. It's an insult!

Because most men don't have the same need for affection as their wives, they often fail to see its relevance, especially when their lives become very busy. But a romantic relationship can't exist without it. That's why it's so important for a husband to maintain an environment of affection for his wife, especially after children arrive. And that environment should reflect her unique interpretation of affection.

another requirement. The behavior must be reasonably enjoyable to become a habit. If you try to practice a behavior that's unpleasant every time you do it, it will never become a stable habit. You'll jump at the first chance you have to avoid doing it.

So as you work through your spouse's list of affectionate behaviors each day, pay close attention to the ones that seem unpleasant, and replace them with more pleasant alternatives. Of course, the replacement behavior must be just as meaningful to your spouse. Otherwise it's not a habit worth forming.

Not surprisingly, affection in a relationship with a member of the opposite sex outside of marriage can easily lead to an affair. It causes such large Love Bank deposits that, when this need is met, the romantic love threshold is usually breached. So your affection should be reserved for each other. Never tell someone of the opposite sex outside of your family how much he or she means to you and how much you care for him or her. It's a formula for marital disaster.

If your marriage has lost its zip, it may have started to lose steam when you stopped being affectionate to each other. But don't despair! You and your spouse can learn to restore it to your relationship. And when you do, you'll find that it makes your marriage fulfilling for both of you.

Sexual Fulfillment

What do you suppose would happen if you were to engage in intimate conversation every day, become each other's favorite recreational companions, and provide the affection that I just described? With all that intimacy, it's likely that both of you would want to make love whenever you had a chance. If you had any sexual problems, they would probably become distant memories. That's because sex thrives in an environment of intimate conversation, recreational companionship, and affection.

But when intimate conversation, recreational companionship, and affection disappear due to life's pressures, especially after children arrive, fulfilling sex usually disappears along with them. Yet most spouses, especially men, expect a passionate sexual relationship in marriage, even when they claim to have no time for the other three needs.

In most marriages one spouse, usually the husband, has a greater need for sex than the other. This fact of life is often played up for amusement in television sitcoms, but in real life, it's not so funny. The husband gets frustrated when he doesn't get the sex he wants, and his frustration usually leads to fights, which makes his wife even less motivated to meet his need. So what can you do to avoid that very unhappy outcome? When your spouse stops meeting your need for sexual fulfillment—or any other intimate emotional need—how can you get what you need from him or her?

I suggest something very similar to what I propose regarding all of the other intimate emotional needs—get into the habit of having a fulfilling sexual relationship. As with intimate conversation, recreational companionship, and affection, you can get into or out of the habit of making love. While it's much easier to make love if you're in the habit of meeting the other three intimate emotional needs, even if you are still trying to form those habits, you should also be getting into the habit of making love. So while you're practicing behavior that will meet the other three needs, I recommend that you also practice meeting the need for sexual fulfillment.

The more you practice any behavior, the quicker you'll get into the habit of doing it. So it's easier to get into the habit of making love if you do it every day, or at least make love whenever you spend a few hours together. In fact, I've found that couples with the most serious sexual problems and inhibitions seem to respond very well to an assignment that requires frequent lovemaking.

But just like anything else, if the way you make love is unpleasant for either of you, practice itself will not get the job done—both of you must enjoy the experience. That means you must both respond to each other sexually every time you make love. But many spouses, particularly women, don't understand their sexual response well enough to know how it is triggered. When they make love, they don't know how to become sexually aroused and experience a climax.

If you are one of those people who are not really sure what it takes to trigger a sexual response, I encourage you to read any one of the scores of books that are written to help improve lovemaking in marriage. I cover this topic in my book, *His Needs, Her Needs: Building an Affair-Proof Marriage*, and its accompanying workbook, *Five Steps to Romantic Love.* Another very helpful book for women who have difficulty reaching a climax is *Women's Orgasm: A Guide to Sexual Satisfaction*, by Georgia Kline-Graber, R.N., and Benjamin Graber, M.D.[1]

The environment created when the other three intimate emotional needs are met goes a long way toward preparing most women for sex, but there are other details that every husband must understand to make sex a good experience for his wife. If she explains to him what makes it enjoyable for her and he follows her advice, she will usually make love to him as often as he would like.

It's easier to meet each other's intimate emotional needs when you're in love. But if you've lost your feeling of love for each other, the fastest way to get it back is to meet these four needs for each other. Don't wait for your love to return before you meet each other's emotional needs. Do it now, because if you wait, your love will probably never be restored. If you get into the habit of meeting all of each other's intimate emotional needs, including sexual fulfillment, it will *trigger* and *maintain* your feeling of love.

Shortcuts Don't Work

As I mentioned before, men and women don't usually see romance the same way. Women tend to envision romance as acts of heartfelt affection and deep, intimate conversation. Men, on the other hand, tend to think of romance as having sex with a woman who is his favorite recreational companion. The truth is that romance is about all of those things because they all fulfill intimate emotional needs. And to keep a romantic relationship

45

alive, the expectations of both husband and wife should be met simultaneously.

But most couples strive for efficiency in life, especially after the children arrive, and romance is often its victim. In an effort to cut corners, men spend less time engaged in affection and intimate conversation with their wife, and women try to do with less sex and recreation with their husband. Instead of creating a romantic relationship that is mutually fulfilling, they both eliminate the parts they feel are less important. And when that happens, romance comes to an abrupt end.

Maintaining romantic love isn't rocket science, but strangely enough, some of the smartest people on earth haven't figured this one out. They think that romance is a mystery, something that comes and goes by pure chance. Or they think it's unsustainable—that within a year or two every romantic relationship is doomed to fade away.

They're wrong. The feeling of love is scientifically predictable. And it's not controlled by Cupid—it's controlled by the way a man and woman treat each other. When they fulfill each other's intimate emotional needs, their love for each other can last indefinitely. And when they try to take shortcuts, it dies away.

Love Takes Time

Try to remember how much time you spent with each other prior to marriage. What did you do with that time? If you are like most couples, you spent at least fifteen hours each week together in person or on the telephone, and you used that time to meet each other's intimate emotional needs. That's what it takes to maintain a romantic relationship—enough time to meet intimate emotional needs.

The primary reason that couples lose their love for each other is that they stop meeting each other's intimate emotional needs. And the primary reason they stop meeting those needs is that they don't think they have time to meet them. Other priorities, such as children and careers, squeeze out the time a couple should be spending in intimate conversation, recreational companionship, intimate affection, and sexual fulfillment.

I've done considerable research into the minimum amount of time it takes to meet those four intimate emotional needs. Remember the amount of time I mentioned above when you thought back to your dating days? Fifteen hours a week. It turns out that's the amount of time it takes for the average couple to sustain a successful romantic relationship. And that time must be scheduled every week. You might think it seems contrived to actually schedule time to meet your spouse's intimate emotional needs, but again, think back to when you dated. That's precisely how it happened then—you scheduled time to be with each other.

Now that you're married and are together every day, it's easy to assume such scheduling isn't required—that simply being in the house together or being asleep in bed together will get the job done. But it's not so. Only when you give each other your *undivided* attention are you able to meet intimate emotional needs. And you will not find time to give each other undivided attention unless it's planned. So I recommend that every Sunday afternoon at 3:30, you and your spouse sit down together and schedule fifteen hours for undivided attention during the week.

The sole purpose of the time you schedule should be to meet the four intimate emotional needs that we discussed in this chapter. You should be alone—or at least your children should be asleep—during those fifteen hours. And you must be awake and alert. Don't try scheduling

47

Six Other Important Emotional Needs

I've focused primary attention on the four intimate emotional needs because you'll make each other the happiest when you meet them—you'll make the largest Love Bank deposits. But there are six other important emotional needs that should also be met in marriage: admiration, domestic support, family commitment, financial support, honesty and openness, and physical attractiveness.

If you want more information on these six needs, read my book *His Needs, Her Needs: Building an Affair-Proof Marriage* (Revell, 2001) and its accompanying workbook, *Five Steps to Romantic Love* (Revell, 2002). While I strongly recommend that you put your greatest effort and emphasis on meeting the intimate emotional needs for each other, these other six important emotional needs should not be ignored. They're all part of what it means to provide extraordinary care.

that time to be together when you're exhausted at the end of a busy day.

If it seems impossible to find fifteen hours in your week to give undivided attention to your spouse, consider this: You have 112 waking hours each week to use however you please (7 twenty-four-hour days gives you 168 total hours, and 7 days with 8 hours of sleep at night takes 56 hours away, leaving 112 hours). Time to get ready for the day and time to get ready to sleep should take about 12 hours, and work should not take more than another 50 hours. That leaves 50 hours for everything else that's important. And the time it takes to meet each other's intimate emotional needs is most important. It's what you promised each other when you married, and it's what you expect in marriage. It's an essential part of extraordinary care.

When you were married, you promised to care for each other in joy and in sorrow, in sickness and in health, in plenty and in want, as long as you both shall live. What that really means is that you promised each other *romance* in spite of your circumstances. You committed to exclusively fulfill each other's most intimate emotional needs, and you didn't say "until children do us part."

If the romance in your marriage is slipping or is gone altogether, the clock is ticking. Sooner or later, one or both of you will crave romantic attention. Some try to find that fulfillment in an affair, and others simply divorce. But you can avoid those disasters by simply keeping romance alive in your own marriage—and you do that by meeting each other's intimate emotional needs.

4

How to Avoid Making Each Other Unhappy

Love Busters

The most basic ingredient of traditional marriage is the extraordinary care that a husband and wife provide each other. If they meet each other's important emotional needs, they've gone a long way toward providing that care. And it helps them make huge deposits in their Love Bank accounts—deposits that sustain their feeling of love for each other.

But there's more to extraordinary care than just making each other happy. It also requires an effort to avoid making each other unhappy. As it turns out, even if you're successful in making your spouse happy by meeting important emotional needs, you're also likely to make your spouse miserable if you don't collar some very destructive predispositions that we all share. I call those predispositions Love Busters, because that's what they do—they destroy romantic love.

If your spouse has been complaining about the way you treat him or her, it's time to confront Love Busters. By meeting each other's important emotional needs, you'll be each other's greatest source of happiness. But if Love Busters are left unchecked, you'll also become the greatest source of each other's unhappiness. That's why your extraordinary care should not only make your spouse happy, but it should also prevent you from making your spouse unhappy.

What Are Love Busters?

A Love Buster is any habit that makes your spouse unhappy. While a single thoughtless act is bad enough, a thoughtless habit is much worse because it's repeated. Love Busters are relentless, causing enough Love Bank withdrawals over time to threaten your love for each other.

A lack of empathy is usually at the core of Love Busters—we don't feel the pain we inflict on each other. That's what I always seem to battle when I encourage one spouse to avoid doing anything that would hurt the other spouse. Each spouse complains about how thoughtless the other one is, without much awareness of his or her own thoughtlessness.

For example, you may find it extremely rude that your spouse ignores you when you come home from work. But have you considered how rude it is to come home late without so much as a phone call? Since we don't feel the pain we cause others, it's easy to focus on what bothers us and ignore what bothers others.

When one spouse complains about the other's thoughtlessness, instead of apologizing and promising to avoid it in the future, the offending spouse often does more damage by trying to justify the offense: "You shouldn't feel that way," or "I had a right to do what I did." If the offending spouse had felt the pain that was inflicted, there would be no excuses—no effort to explain away the offense. Instead there would be an immediate willingness and effort to avoid the problem in the future.

If I could just switch a couple's awareness for one week so that each would feel what the other person feels, Love Busters would be easy to overcome. Both spouses would understand the foolishness of their excuses because no amount of justification alleviates the suffering they cause.

But because we don't feel the pain we inflict, we can let Love Busters grow until we become impossible to live with. Even if we have the ability to meet our spouse's intimate emotional needs, our spouse eventually decides it isn't worth it. And our Love Bank balance becomes so overdrawn that instead of being loved, we're hated.

In marriage, there are a host of ways that spouses make each other unhappy. But I've found that they all fall into six categories: selfish demands, disrespectful judgments, angry outbursts, dishonesty, annoying habits, and independent behavior. It's easy to justify all of these Love Busters, especially since you don't feel their negative impact. You may regard a demand as simply encouraging your spouse to do what he or she should have done all along, disrespect as helping your spouse gain a proper perspective on life, and angry outbursts as a way to express your deepest emotions. Maybe you've convinced yourself that dishonesty protects your spouse or that your annoying habits and independent behavior are just part of who you are.

Yet all of these excuses ignore one basic fact: you make your spouse unhappy whenever you engage in these thoughtless acts. And whenever your spouse is unhappy,

Love Bank withdrawals are taking place. So if you want to protect your love for each other, take some time to pinpoint which Love Busters have infected your marriage, and then create a plan to throw them out. It's essential housecleaning if you are to provide extraordinary care in marriage.

Selfish Demands

When you request something you need from your spouse and the request is denied or ignored, what are you tempted to do next? For most of us, a denied request prompts a more forceful measure—making a demand to get what we want.

For example, consider a wife who sees her husband sitting on the couch watching television as she's cleaning up the kitchen after dinner. "Get up and give me some help! Can't you hear the baby crying?" she might call to her husband. And that demand seems reasonable, doesn't it? After all, the husband should be more helpful. But it's still a Love Buster.

Or think about this scenario: A husband finds that his wife has run up a credit card bill that blows their budget sky high. "If you can't be responsible with a credit card, you don't deserve to have one. Give it to me right now!" he demands. Doesn't he have a point? Maybe so, but he's destroying her love for him with his demand.

Making demands is a predisposition that almost all of us seem to have at birth, and it's so automatic that most people ignore the fact that demands make them very unpleasant to be around. People easily overlook how ineffective demands are—they usually fail to get the job done. Instead of encouraging our spouse to do whatever it is we want him or her to do for us, making a demand actually makes him or her less likely to do it for us next time. The lazy husband is less likely to give his wife the help she needs. The spendthrift wife is less likely to become more responsible with her credit card.

Nobody likes to be told what to do. Yet when *we* make demands, we feel justified—it seems like a reasonable way to get what we need. But if we could actually feel the effect our demands have on our spouse, we wouldn't make them because we certainly don't want our spouse making demands of us.

Without a doubt, you and your spouse should get the help and cooperation that you need from each other—you should share the burdens of life. But demands don't work. They make you selfish, controlling, and abusive. Instead of getting the help you need, they prompt your spouse to avoid you as much as possible. Do you want help, or do you want to drive your spouse away?

Marriage isn't like the army; there are no sergeants and no privates. Neither you nor your spouse has a right to tell the other what to do. And when you try to do so, you create a temporary solution at best. Your spouse may fulfill one demand, but what happens the next time the problem surfaces? Your spouse will give greater resistance, and your desires will become increasingly difficult to obtain. Demands and other forms of manipulation don't build cooperation; they build resentment and resistance.

So what's the alternative to selfish demands? It's thoughtful requests—getting what you need from each other by simply explaining what you'd like and asking your spouse how he or she would feel fulfilling your request. If your spouse thinks the request will be unpleasant to fulfill, then, instead of trying to force your spouse to do it anyway, discuss ways he or she could help you that wouldn't be unpleasant.

"I've already tried that, and it doesn't work," may be your immediate reaction. "What if my spouse just doesn't want to help?" That's where negotiation takes over. In the next chapter I'll give you some tips on how you and your spouse can become skilled negotiators. But for now, I want you to be aware of the fact that demands will not solve your problems. They actually create a new problem—you become a controlling and abusive spouse.

Disrespectful Judgments

Disrespectful judgments are usually cleverly disguised demands—and another effort to get what we want. When an outright demand doesn't work, we try to convince our spouse that his or her failure to do something we want is a personal shortcoming. So we try to "straighten out" our spouse.

For example, if our spouse doesn't spend as much time watching the kids as we'd like, we'll call him or her a bad parent. All we really want is some help taking care of the children, but when our demands won't work, we turn to personal attacks. Without a doubt, demands are abusive, but disrespectful judgments can make demands seem merciful by comparison.

These attacks aren't necessarily intended to be mean-spirited. We often rationalize our disrespect by convincing ourselves that we're doing our spouse a favor. If he or she would only see the light of our superior opinion, we tell ourselves, he or she would be much happier. We're just pointing out a personal flaw to help him or her become a better person.

But even if we did have pure motives, using disrespectful judgments is still a controlling and abusive strategy. It's controlling because it imposes our point of view on our spouse, and it's abusive because it causes our spouse to be very unhappy. When we try to impose our opinions and values on our spouse, we imply that he or she has poor judgment. And that's disrespectful. We may not say this in so many words, but it's the clear message he or she hears. If we valued our spouse's judgment more, we would question our own opinions and values.

Disrespectful judgments are personally threatening, arrogant, and rude. And they make sizable withdrawals from the Love Bank.

I'm not saying that you shouldn't disagree with your spouse. But I want to encourage you to *respectfully* disagree. Present your point of view as an opinion, not a fact. And explain why you have that opinion. Then try to understand your spouse's opinion and the reasoning behind it, avoiding ridicule at all costs. Entertain the possibility that you might be wrong and your spouse might be right. As you come to understand each other's opinions and reasoning, you not only get to know each other better, but you have the opportunity to change each other's opinions. That's how respectful persuasion works.

You and your spouse each bring both wisdom and foolishness into your marriage. By sharing your opinions and sorting through their advantages and disadvantages respectfully, you can create a new perspective on life that's superior to what either of you could have had alone. But if you're disrespectful toward each other, you'll not only fail to gain from each other's wisdom, but you'll also destroy your love for each other.

Test for Disrespect

When we're being disrespectful, we often fail to recognize it ourselves. We think we're being helpful when we're actually being hurtful. And all we feel is our own self-righteous belief that we're doing the right thing. So how can you know if you're a perpetrator of disrespectful judgments? The simplest way to find out is to ask your spouse. You can't feel the effect of your disrespect, but he or she can.

If your spouse identifies you as someone who makes disrespectful judgments, you may be tempted to make yet another disrespectful judgment and claim that he or she is wrong! Resist that temptation at all costs because in every case of abuse, the victim is a far better judge of its existence than the perpetrator. Take his or her word for it, and start working on a plan to eliminate disrespect.

57

Disrespectful judgments don't belong in your marriage. They don't solve problems—they only create resentment and destroy love. So if this Love Buster has invaded your marriage, try replacing it with respectful persuasion.

Angry Outbursts

Marriage has gotten a bad rap in some circles today, and Love Busters are the reason. Some people have claimed that marriage traps women into a life of some very unpleasant experiences. These people see marriage as an opportunity for husbands to dominate, control, and abuse their wives.

It's true that there is a risk of domestic abuse in marriage. Some women are the victims of brutal assault by their husbands, and some husbands are assaulted by their wives. But research has shown that the biggest risk for domestic abuse isn't actually found in marriages—it is found in nonmarital domestic arrangements. In most marriages, particularly in traditional marriages, couples realize that they are obligated to provide a level of care to each other that's not expected in nonmarital cohabitation. And that extraordinary care forms a protective shield for married women.

But not every marriage is a traditional marriage. There are some who have not kept their commitment to care for each other and to protect each other from destructive instincts and habits. They let their instinct to have angry outbursts run amok, putting their spouse in grave danger.

When spouses allow themselves to become so angry that they become physically violent, permanent injury and even death await their loved one. I've counseled hundreds of people who have inflicted serious injuries on their spouse, and I'm grateful to legislators and law enforcers who have made it clear that we will not tolerate such behavior. Putting perpetrators of such abuse into prison for their behavior is often one of the best tools that therapists like myself have at our disposal. With the threat of incarceration, we've been able to get the attention of these offenders and help them overcome this most dangerous Love Buster.

But physical violence isn't the only way that angry outbursts are expressed. And physical damage isn't the only kind of damage inflicted by an angry outburst. In fact, spouses who are not in physical danger are often in serious emotional danger because of the *verbal* abuse they suffer during an attack.

I've witnessed firsthand the effects of verbal abuse. Clients who have been the victim of angry outbursts have shown both physical and emotional symptoms characteristic of prolonged stress. They tend to be more depressed, more anxious, and more likely to blame themselves for most of the problems they face. And that's the purpose of an angry outburst—to blame someone for failing to do what you demand and to punish him or her for it.

> ### Report It
>
> Every incident of physical abuse should be reported to the police. Even a slap across the face should be reported. When physical abuse is kept secret, it grows just like mold in a closet and becomes increasingly dangerous. But when it is made public to law enforcement, the perpetrator is forced to recognize the seriousness of the problem and is forced to do something about it. Some of the most successful outcomes I've witnessed have been with a spouse who has already spent time in jail and is at risk to spend even more time behind bars unless the angry outbursts are eliminated completely.

When demands don't produce results and disrespect doesn't work either, people often resort to angry outbursts. And since demands and disrespect don't generally get the job done, an angry outburst usually appears with them. Together these three make up the framework of a typical argument. All three of these strategies are abusive,

Zero Tolerance Policy

Angry outbursts should not be tolerated in marriage. Even words spoken in anger should be eliminated. Yet there are many who simply can't seem to stop losing their temper. If that describes you, I recommend professional anger management training.

A successful anger management program begins with personal counseling designed to convince you that your anger is not the fault of anyone else, especially your spouse. Unless you hold yourself totally responsible for your anger, controlling it is hopeless.

After being fully convinced that no one has the right to hurt anyone else in anger, you'll be ready to learn how to get your angry outbursts under control. In a support group, you will learn relaxation techniques to apply under stress, acceptable ways to avoid frustration, and effective negotiating skills. For many, a weekly support group is usually essential for a full recovery, which may take as long as two years.

If your spouse is the victim of your angry outbursts, you are not providing extraordinary care—you do not have a traditional marriage. There is no legitimate excuse for angry outbursts in marriage. Practice a zero tolerance policy when it comes to this Love Buster.

controlling, and tragic. And when spouses unleash them on each other, they become the greatest source of each other's unhappiness.

Although anger is nothing more than an abusive way to get what we want—or punish someone for not giving us what we want—our instincts try to convince us that we have the right to be angry. We feel that someone is deliberately making us unhappy (by not giving us what we want), and that isn't fair. In our angry state, we're convinced that the offender will keep upsetting us until he or she is taught a lesson. Since the person has not listened to reason (demands and disrespect), he or she deserves to be punished.

Anger seems to offer a simple solution to our problem—just destroy the troublemaker. But if that supposed troublemaker is our spouse, we hurt the one we've promised to protect. When we're angry, we don't care about our spouse's feelings, and we're willing to turn from extraordinary care to extraordinary harm.

In the end, we have nothing to gain from an angry outburst. Punishment doesn't solve marital problems—it makes them worse. When we become angry with our spouse, we threaten his or her safety and security. If our spouse is emotionally strong, he or she rises to the challenge and tries to destroy us in retaliation—or becomes so disgusted that he or she leaves us. If our spouse is emotionally weak, we contribute to that weakness. Either way, when anger wins, love always loses.

You'll lose your spouse's love if you use the abusive and controlling strategies of demands, disrespect, and anger to try to get what you need. And you won't get what you need. But if you learn how to resolve conflicts with thoughtful requests and respectful persuasion, you'll solve each problem once and for all. The extraordinary care provided in traditional marriage gets the job done.

Dishonesty

Our instincts try to convince us that there's nothing wrong with demands, disrespect, or anger in marriage. They also try to convince us that there's nothing wrong with being dishonest once in a while. But dishonesty is wrong for the same reason the first three Love Busters are wrong—it causes unhappiness in marriage. Whenever you tell a lie, and your spouse discovers it, your Love Bank balance takes a significant hit.

But dishonesty is a strange Love Buster. Obviously, no one likes dishonesty, but sometimes honesty seems

What about Little White Lies?

I'll admit that infidelity is an extreme example of something you might be tempted to lie about. But "little white lies" can be just as destructive when discovered, and there's much less justification for them. If it makes sense to be honest about something as hurtful as an affair, it makes even more sense to be honest about something more trivial, such as buying something that your spouse doesn't feel you can afford.

even more damaging. What if the truth is more painful than a lie?

When a wife first learns that her husband has been unfaithful, the pain is often so great that she wishes she had been left ignorant. A husband has the same reaction when he discovers his wife's affair—it's like a knife in his heart, and he wonders if it would have been better not to know. In fact, many marriage counselors advise clients to avoid telling spouses about past infidelity, saying that it's too painful for people to handle. Besides, if it's over and done with, why dredge up the sewage of the past?

It's this sort of confusion that leads some of the most well-intentioned husbands and wives to lie to each other or at least give each other false impressions. They feel that dishonesty will help them protect each other's feelings. Honesty, on the other hand, would be cruel in some instances.

But dishonesty, as well-intentioned as it may be, creates an emotional barrier between a husband and wife. It's something hidden—a secret that can't be mentioned. Yet it's right under the surface of every conversation.

Also, dishonesty can be as addictive as a drug. One lie leads to another. If you start using dishonesty to protect each other's feelings, where will it end?

When the lie is eventually exposed and the truth is revealed, the knowledge that your spouse has lied to you is devastating. What can you believe? If your spouse has lied once, can you believe anything he or she says? Trust, which is so essential in marriage, is destroyed.

Dishonesty strangles compatibility. To create and sustain a compatible relationship, you must know as much about each other as possible. You must be honest about your thoughts, feelings, habits, likes, dislikes, personal history, daily activities, and plans for the future. When misinformation is part of the mix, you have little hope of making successful adjustments to each other.

Honesty helps *build* compatibility and love because it tends to make our behavior more thoughtful. If we knew that everything we do and say would be televised and reviewed by our spouse each day, we'd be far less likely to engage in thoughtless acts. And honesty is like the television camera in our lives. If we're honest about what we do, we tend to be more likely to consider our spouse's feelings before we act.

In an honest relationship, thoughtless acts are usually corrected. Bad habits are identified and nipped in the bud. And couples eliminate incompatible attitudes and behavior before they grow out of control.

If you have a tendency to lie or distort the truth, you're probably harboring a host of bad habits that should be exposed and chased out of your marriage before they ruin your love for each other. Be *radically* honest with each other, and start today. It's an important way to demonstrate your extraordinary care for each other.

Annoying Habits

With our current cultural emphasis on tolerance, this next Love Buster, annoying habits, takes a bit of explaining. Our instincts are already encouraging us to do whatever we please, and now they have support for it in our schools! We are encouraged to accept others for who they are and what they do, even when what they do is incredibly annoying.

While accepting other people's annoying habits may be possible when we don't have much contact with them, to *live* with them is another matter entirely. And when it comes to being in love with that person, annoying habits must be dealt with or else romantic love doesn't stand a chance.

Our personal mannerisms—such as the way we eat, the way we clean up after ourselves (or don't!), and the way we talk—can be annoying. But they often get the short shrift in marriage because it's assumed that they're a part of us that can't be changed. We assume that our spouse should be able to shrug it off and accept us as we are. But our spouse can't ignore our annoying habits. It's like the steady drip-drip of water torture. Annoying habits can nickel-and-dime our Love Bank account into bankruptcy.

When our behavior annoys our spouse, we tend to ignore the problem. After all, it doesn't annoy us, so why should it annoy anyone else? But when *we* are the ones being annoyed, we see the problem from a very different perspective. We usually feel that something should be done to correct the problem—immediately! This is particularly so when we've explained that the behavior bothers us and yet it continues to go on. It's not just the behavior itself but the thought behind it—the idea that our spouse doesn't care enough about us to stop doing it.

As I've already mentioned, lack of empathy is at the root of the problem. If Joe were to become Jane for a day and Jane became Joe—if they could only know what it feels like to experience their own annoying behavior—they would be much more motivated to change.

But since we cannot feel what our spouse feels, we are left with the meaning of extraordinary care as our sole motivation for eliminating our own annoying behavior. By promising your spouse that you will avoid making him or her unhappy, you are also promising to eliminate your annoying behavior. And it can be done. All your habits can change, including those that your spouse finds annoying. Even better, when you replace an annoying habit with an attractive habit, the new habit becomes just as effortless, and just as much a part of you, as the annoying habit it replaces. All it takes is repeating the new behavior often enough for it to become a habit.

Remember, whenever you do something that bothers your spouse, whether it's intentional or unintentional, you're making Love Bank withdrawals. Those annoying habits that don't seem so important are destroying your spouse's love for you. The complaints you hear (and find annoying) are really cries for help. When you tell your spouse to stop complaining and to just accept you as you are, you fail to understand the damage you're doing to your Love Bank account. For this reason, complaining is the only annoying habit that I encourage couples to keep.

If I've convinced you that your annoying habits can drain a Love Bank account, you may wonder where you should begin in trying to eliminate them. After all, there may be many.

I suggest that you chip away at them systematically. Each spouse should make a list of the habits that annoy him or her most. Then put them in order of how annoying they are, with the most annoying habits first. As you look at your spouse's list, you may find that some habits can be easily eliminated—all it will take is a decision to end them, and they're a thing of the past. After eliminating those habits, the ones that remain each will require an individual plan. So only take on three of the remaining habits at a time, from the top of the list down. When those three are overcome, create plans to eliminate the next three. Even if you do not eventually overcome every annoying habit, you will have eliminated the worst ones, and your spouse will give you credit for making yourself much more attractive. It's what we expect of someone who provides extraordinary care.

Independent Behavior

I've been impressed by the large number of books on marriage that encourage couples to live independent lives. These books encourage couples to have different friends, different recreational activities, and different hobbies as well as to make their decisions independently. In fact, they actually discourage spouses from trying to blend their lives together. Of course, most of the authors of these books have been divorced at least once. Take it from a successful marital therapist who is still in love with his first wife of forty-two years, independent behavior is a Love Buster—it destroys romantic love and destroys marriages.

Are you making some of your decisions as if your spouse doesn't exist? Do you bother to ask how he or she feels about your plans? Or do you just go ahead and do what you please? If you ignore your spouse's feelings when you make some of your plans, you've invited our sixth Love Buster into your marriage—independent behavior.

This Love Buster represents any activity that fails to take your spouse's feelings and interests into account. Unlike annoying habits that are performed without thought, independent behavior is planned—you usually even schedule it! Going back to our lack of empathy, it's easy to make the mistake of independent behavior because you don't feel your spouse's pain. You feel fine when your plans ignore your spouse's feelings. Your only clue that it might be a bad idea is that your spouse is complaining bitterly.

Since the 1960s, we've been given lots of excuses for independent behavior. We've been encouraged to take better care of ourselves and ignore the feelings of others. We're taught to say: "You're not my mother (or father).

Stop trying to control me! Why should I have to have your permission for something I want to do?"

The answer to that question, of course, is that the issue is not about control—it's about thoughtfulness. You're being controlled when someone forces you to do something that's good for him or her and bad for you. But thoughtfulness is entirely different. You're being thoughtful when you decide *not* to do something that's good for you and bad for your spouse. And that gets at the heart of what independent behavior really is—it's thoughtlessness. It's running roughshod over the feelings of your spouse so you can be a little happier.

It isn't permission that thoughtful spouses seek—it's making sure that every decision is in the couple's mutual interest instead of being in the interest of only one of them. When you marry, you should be thinking about *both* of you when you make decisions. They should be made interdependently, not independently, because you are no longer two separate individuals—you are now partners. Your spouse is connected to you, and he or she feels the effects of almost everything you decide to do.

An independent behavior here and there is bad enough. But if you make lifestyle decisions independently, such as your career, the house you buy, the way you raise your children, or the church you attend, your marriage will be on the rocks in no time. The choices you make to create the fabric of your lives together should make both of you happy. Otherwise, you'll find yourselves being dragged into a way of life that at least one of you can't tolerate. That person will wake up each morning dreading the day because it wasn't designed with him or her in mind—a victim of thoughtless decisions on a grand scale. That's why it's so important to make all of your decisions together, especially lifestyle decisions.

Because independent behavior is at the root of a couple's failure to create a mutually enjoyable lifestyle, we'll continue to discuss this sixth Love Buster in the next chapter, which focuses special attention on this third aspect of extraordinary care.

Tolerating Love Busters: Double Trouble

If you think about it, failure to avoid Love Busters can be a greater disaster in marriage than the failure to meet each other's intimate emotional needs. Once you unleash them on your spouse, his or her desire to meet your intimate emotional needs evaporates, and your spouse won't even want you to meet his or her needs. So Love Busters are double trouble: they make Love Bank withdrawals and prevent Love Bank deposits.

For more information about these six Love Busters, read my book *Love Busters: Overcoming Habits That Destroy Romantic Love* (Revell, 2002), and its accompanying workbook *Five Steps to Romantic Love* (Revell, 2002).

Are Love Busters threatening your marriage? If they're just starting to creep in, you may have a hard time recognizing them for the monsters they are. But if you've struggled with Love Busters for a while, your Love Banks may be running on empty. In either case, there's no time like the present to eliminate them.

Love Busters don't belong in marriage. They keep you from having what you really want from your marriage and from life itself. And they represent an obvious failure to provide each other the extraordinary care that you expect and deserve.

5

How to Create a Mutually Enjoyable Lifestyle

The Policy of Joint Agreement

My life was to be a great adventure. I would travel throughout the world, get a taste of just about everything I could think of seeing and doing, and Joyce, the love of my life, would join me in that adventure. It was my dream.

But after marrying Joyce, I discovered that my dream would have been a nightmare to her. Her dream was raising a family in one place that she could call home. Traveling from one country to another was the very last thing she wanted to do with her life.

As it turned out, my dream didn't make much sense if Joyce was to be my life partner. My dream had to become our dream. We tried moving around the country a few times, but it soon became clear that if Joyce were to be happy, we couldn't be world travelers.

Since Joyce, not travel, was the most important part of my dream, we had to come up with a new adventure that could make both of us happy. And the one we finally developed turned out to be very different than the one I had first envisioned. It involved travel, but after each trip, we returned to our home in the Twin Cities.

I was willing to change my dream to a new dream that would make Joyce's life as happy as mine. But if we had been married just five years later, I would have been encouraged by our culture to make a tragic mistake—to try to fulfill my dream of travel with or without Joyce. Instead of changing my dream to include her feelings and interests, I would have been encouraged to ignore her concerns. The fulfillment of my dreams would have been considered to be far more important than my care for her. Cultural influences would have directed me to travel, and Joyce would have had to either put up with travel or leave me. In either case, we would not have experienced the enjoyable and fulfilling life that we have both spent together.

Joyce and I were married during a period of radical social change. The 1960s saw the end of a culture that valued the care of others and the beginning of a culture that valued the care of oneself. Books, teachers, and even ministers were encouraging people to discover, love, and care for themselves—at the expense of others if necessary. To make the care and consideration of others as important as the care of oneself was judged to be foolish at best and dangerous at worst.

In other words, the culture, and the educational system that supported it, had changed from one that encouraged a happy marriage to one that encouraged marital conflict and divorce. If we had followed the emerging emphasis on self-centeredness, Joyce and I would have spent our lives fulfilling dreams that did not include each other. By now, we would have been divorced.

But we stuck with the traditional values that characterized our generation. That meant we were prepared to provide extraordinary care to each other—even when it meant exchanging our personal dreams for dreams we could pursue together.

How do you and your spouse make lifestyle decisions? Do you let each other know how various alternatives will affect each of you before the decision is final? Do you look for alternatives that will benefit both of you? Or do you tend to discuss a decision after it's already been made—and one of you is strenuously objecting?

If you're like most people, you make your decision and then wait for the fallout. If your spouse doesn't object, you think you've made a good choice. But if your spouse disapproves, you fight about it. You find this approach to be reasonable since you think you have a right to make your own decisions about issues that affect you, right?

But your decisions don't just affect you. They also affect your spouse either positively or negatively. You are either making Love Bank deposits or withdrawals with every decision you make. If you care about your spouse and want him or her to be in love with you, you should make decisions that have a positive impact on your account. And you do that by making decisions that satisfy both of you.

Creating a mutually enjoyable lifestyle is the caring thing to do. Why live a life that's good for you and bad for your spouse? The only reason you might even be tempted to do such an uncaring thing is that you don't feel what your spouse feels. You may think you should have the right to choose your vocation, your hobbies, your church, or your car without considering the feelings of your spouse. But if you felt the way your spouse feels,

71

you'd make your decision the right way—by making sure your spouse is as enthusiastic about it as you are. Besides, any of your decisions that hurt your spouse will destroy your romantic relationship and, ultimately, destroy your marriage.

Unfortunately, many people believe that if they can't make independent decisions, they can't live productive lives. Even if it does ruin a romantic relationship, to do otherwise would cripple them and cause them to lose their very identity. And don't independent decisions in marriage actually make spouses more desirable to each other? Who wants to be married to someone who's clingy and dependent—unable to make any of his or her own decisions? Isn't an independently minded spouse far more attractive?

All the rationalization in the world cannot overcome the fact that independent decisions ruin marriages. As I've said before, almost everything you and your spouse do in marriage will affect each other to some degree. That's even true of what you do when you are away from each other. But some people have trouble believing that fact. They think that what they do at work, for example, has no effect on their spouse one way or another. After all, their spouse isn't there and doesn't even know what's going on. Yet my job as a marriage counselor has convinced me that some of the decisions most harmful to marriage begin at work. Decisions regarding scheduling at work often prevent spouses from having enough time to meet each other's intimate emotional needs. And decisions that lead to intimate relationships with co-workers have a disastrous impact on your relationship with your spouse.

Trust me, nearly everything you decide to do will eventually make either deposits or withdrawals from your spouse's Love Bank. So if you want to protect your love for each other, you should know how your decisions affect each other before you actually make them, even when you are not together. And the only way to know that crucial fact is to ask.

Independent decisions lead to the sixth Love Buster we discussed in the last chapter—independent behavior. It's a Love Buster because it runs roughshod over the interests and feelings of your spouse. Unless decisions are made to take your spouse's feelings into account, they will drain the Love Bank dry.

There's a far superior alternative to independent behavior that helps spouses create a mutually enjoyable lifestyle. I call that alternative *interdependent* behavior— taking each other's feelings into account before doing anything.

Interdependent Behavior = Extraordinary Care

Because independent behavior ignores your spouse's interests, it's likely to make him or her unhappy for two reasons. First, the thoughtless act itself is a Love Buster. Whenever you do something that's good for you and bad for your spouse, like leaving your spouse at home with the children while you go out to have a good time with your friends, Love Bank withdrawals are inevitable.

Second, by ignoring your spouse's interests, he or she will conclude that you don't care. If you really cared about your spouse, you would work out an agreement in advance that takes your spouse's feelings into account.

Interdependent behavior solves both of these problems. It prevents you from doing anything that hurts your spouse, and it communicates your care by requiring his or her agreement before acting. But it does more than just provide care for your spouse. It also provides care

73

for you. It's a way for both of you to care for each other simultaneously.

Interdependent behavior is a way of saying, "I care about you, and I don't want to do anything that will hurt you. But I also care about how I feel. So let's do what works for both of us." It enables you to stay in love with each other because it leads to behavior that makes deposits into *both* of your Love Banks. It also creates the best environment for your children—one in which they learn to be thoughtful of others by watching you make thoughtful decisions.

When you and your spouse make decisions that take each other into account, you provide the extraordinary care that you expected on the day of your wedding. Isn't that true? Didn't you think that you'd be consulting with each other on decisions that had to be made? Didn't you expect your lifestyle to be a blending of each other's interests? Of course you did. And what you expected is what you should deliver to each other.

No matter what anyone says, it *is* possible to make every decision with your spouse's interest in mind. And it's crucial to do that if you want a marriage that sustains your love for each other. But it's not easy. You'll need some help. And the help I recommend comes in the form of a rule.

The Policy of Joint Agreement—A Rule That Creates Interdependent Behavior

Independent behavior is so pervasive in American marriages that most couples need a rule to keep them from hurting each other. So I've written that rule for all of my clients to follow. It helps them learn to create a mutually enjoyable lifestyle by becoming interdependent. If you follow this rule, you will provide the extraordinary care you promised on the day of your marriage because it will force you to take each other's feelings into account whenever you make decisions. After you both get into the habit of keeping this rule, independent behavior will be completely eliminated from your marriage. I call this rule the **Policy of Joint Agreement**: *Never do anything without an enthusiastic agreement between you and your spouse.*

So what do you think? Does that sound crazy?

As I'll explain in the next chapter, interdependence goes against our instincts and our culture, so people often think this rule is insane when they first read it. But those who follow the rule for a while come to recognize it as the breakthrough they've needed to make their marriage mutually fulfilling. And they realize that their romantic relationship would be impossible to sustain without it.

The Policy of Joint Agreement gives you an opportunity to resolve conflicts the right way—the way that takes the interests of both of you into account simultaneously. Not only is this the caring thing to do, but the final decisions that result are usually wiser than any decision you would have made on your own. By joining together to make each decision, you're able to consider a much broader range of options and come to conclusions that take more factors into account.

When I first introduce this rule to clients, it usually triggers two reactions. At first people react to how they feel about being consulted before their spouse makes a decision: "Does this mean that Lisa must ask me how I feel about what she's planning to do before she does it? I think that's a good idea. There's a lot going on in her life that I'd like to know about, and a lot that I wouldn't agree with if I did know. If she'd tell me her plans in advance and give me the right to veto some of them, I think we'd get along a lot better."

But it doesn't take long for a second reaction to un-fold—how they feel about being required to have their spouse's agreement before they can do anything: "It would be ridiculous to let Lisa keep me from doing what I have to do. Sometimes she just doesn't understand, and so I have to make decisions she doesn't like. I don't think her 'feelings' should keep me from achieving my personal goals."

This takes us back to the problem of empathy. We each want our spouse to be thoughtful of our feelings, but we tend to ignore our spouse's feelings. If we were emotionally connected to each other so that we would feel what each other feels, we'd behave very differently. We'd want to know how our behavior would affect each other—in advance—so we could avoid any discomfort to ourselves. And that's precisely what the Policy of Joint Agreement does. It gives us advance notice of how we will be affecting each other. While we can't actually feel the pain we inflict on each other, it forces us to behave as if we did.

"How Do You Feel?"

The Policy of Joint Agreement helps you become sensi-tive to each other's feelings, especially when you don't feel like doing so. Since you're required to have each other's enthusiastic agreement before you do anything, it forces you to ask each other a very important question: "How do you feel about what I would like to do?"

That simple question and its answer help you build a crucial understanding of each other. You may not actu-ally feel what your spouse feels, but at least you give your spouse the opportunity to inform you. Then, even when you find yourself in a thoughtless mood, the Policy of Joint Agreement forces you to be thoughtful.

You are now a team, not two independent individuals. You should work together to achieve objectives that benefit both of you simultaneously. Why should one of you consider your own interests so important that you can run roughshod over the interests of the other? That's a formula for marital disaster.

When I first see a couple in marital crisis, they are usually living their lives as if their spouse hardly exists—making thoughtless decisions regularly because they don't care how the other feels. As a result, when I introduce the Policy of Joint Agreement, it seems totally irrational to them. They've created a way of life that is based on so many inconsiderate habits that the policy seems to threaten their very existence. At first, they don't want to abandon their thoughtless and insensitive lifestyle. But the more they try following the policy, the easier it becomes to reach agreement. They replace thoughtless decisions with those that take each other's feelings into account. And they develop real compatibility—building a way of life that is comfortable for both of them.

I think you can see why independent behavior ruins a marriage. It not only creates massive Love Bank withdrawals, but it also proves that spouses don't really care about each other. If they did care, they would be thoughtful of each other—they would make decisions that take each other's feelings into account.

It's easy to see why so many people are disillusioned by marriage. I'd be disillusioned too if Joyce were to ignore my feelings when she makes decisions. But that's not the way marriage has to be. And it's certainly not the way it's been in our marriage. By making our decisions together, we demonstrate our extraordinary care for each other, and as a result, our marriage continues to be very fulfilling for both of us.

Government 101

When a husband and wife first marry and are still in love with each other, they tend to make decisions the right way by taking each other's feelings into account. The Policy of Joint Agreement tends to reign for a while, even though most couples are unaware that they are following it. Intimate conversation builds understanding, and that, in turn, helps make decisions mutually advantageous.

But it doesn't take long before the pressures of life make it tempting to scrap bilateral decisions in favor of unilateral decisions. Instead of negotiating to reach mutually acceptable solutions to problems, one spouse, usually the husband, decides that he must make the final decisions. He begins to use the Dictator Strategy to solve problems. This strategy assumes that one spouse has the right, wisdom, and compassion to make decisions correctly. While the other spouse can lobby to have him take her interests into account, when a decision is made, it's final.

Selfish demands prevail when the Dictator Strategy is in force. If one spouse tells the other what to do, without having come to an agreement first, he or she is making a selfish demand and is using the Dictator Strategy. In the previous chapter I discussed the damage that selfish demands can cause, but it bears repeating: when one spouse thinks he or she has the right to make demands, the loss of love is almost inevitable.

Dictators haven't been known to be particularly wise or compassionate. They tend to make decisions in their own interest and at the expense of their citizens. The same thing happens in marriage. When one spouse is given the right to make all final decisions, the other spouse usually suffers. And their love suffers.

If this strategy is left unchecked, slavery, so feared by feminists, rears its ugly head. Instead of a partnership, a wife finds herself dominated by a dictator. Decades ago some women settled for the Dictator Strategy, but few would today. And they shouldn't. The practice of a husband making unilateral decisions proves to his wife that he really doesn't care about anyone but himself.

And the problem only gets worse from there. I have heard many young wives complain about their husband's decisions to come and go as he pleases, make his own friends, stay out late without letting her know where he is, and other thoughtless acts. At the same time, she is obligated to stay home evenings with their children, cook and clean, and be available to him for sex whenever needed.

Before long these women start to put up a fight. "If he doesn't care about me, why should I care about him?" they reason. So they create the Dueling Dictators Strategy. As resentment grows, the subordinate spouse decides to stage a coup, raising both spouses to dictator status.

Then guess what happens when these two spouses disagree? It's all out war, with each side looking after his or her own interests. After the dust settles, the stronger and more determined spouse wins the decision, which means that his or her solution is put into effect. But the losing dictator is already plotting more carefully for the next battle.

Unfortunately, millions of unhappy couples use the Dueling Dictators Strategy. It makes problem solving unpleasant for all involved, but at least it seems more fair than the Dictator Strategy. After all, no one loses all the time with this strategy. Of course, now instead of one spouse being victimized, both spouses are victimized!

At this point marriage becomes miserable. Couples who experience this often feel as if they have one of only two choices: either they can divorce or they can create a marriage of convenience. To continue in misery is simply not an option.

Those who choose a marriage of convenience begin to use what I call the Anarchy Strategy. This strategy gives up hope of resolving conflict and takes the position, "Every man for himself!" A husband, wife, or sometimes both, do whatever they want and refuse to do anything that their spouse wants. Couples grasp at anarchy as their last resort when the Dueling Dictators Strategy fails. But just like countries in anarchy, anarchic marriages become chaotic and soon fall apart. Ultimately, most of these couples eventually divorce as well.

But there is another way for couples to handle conflict—a way that doesn't destroy their love for each other and doesn't lead to divorce. It's the Democracy Strategy, in which husbands and wives don't make a decision until they're both in agreement. The Democracy Strategy for marital conflict requires unanimous consent. Neither spouse can impose their will on the other.

Unlike all the other strategies we've seen, the Democracy Strategy addresses conflicts and resolves them with no victims. The outcome of every decision is in the best interest of both spouses.

So why isn't the Democracy Strategy used in all, or even most, marriages? Because we aren't born with an instinct for democracy. Instead, we're born with an instinct to get our way at any cost. That attitude puts the Dictator Strategy into play in most marriages. And once that happens, the Dueling Dictator and Anarchy Strategies are often not far behind.

The Democracy Strategy will not seem as natural to you as the others—it requires time and thought. But it's the only sensible way for you to make marital decisions. It not only provides wise solutions to your problems, but it will also draw you much closer to each other emotionally. And that's a basic requirement for every romantic relationship.

The Policy of Joint Agreement makes the Democracy Strategy possible. It gives both spouses equal power and control over the choices that are to be made. *Never do anything without an enthusiastic agreement between you and your spouse*—that simple rule forces you to find a mutually acceptable solution before any action is taken. And how do you find that solution? It's through the fine art of negotiation.

Negotiators, Take Your Places

Democracy isn't easy, and neither is marital negotiation. But for civilization and marriage alike, the rewards found in considering the interests of others are well worth the added effort. So how do you reach an enthusiastic agreement when you and your spouse face a conflict?

The most important first step you must each take is to accept the Policy of Joint Agreement as the rule you will live by for the rest of your lives together. It helps create the question, "How do you feel about what I'd like to do?" Without that question, you'll find yourself making unilateral decisions that will ultimately lead to a miserable marriage or divorce.

When the question is asked and you receive a negative response, the Policy of Joint Agreement offers you two choices: either abandon the idea or try to discover alternative ways of making it possible—with your spouse's enthusiastic agreement. That's where negotiation begins!

With practice, you and your spouse can become experts at getting what you need in ways that create mutual, enthusiastic agreement. Once you agree to this policy, fair negotiation will become a way of life for you. And you'll also be forced to abandon demands, disrespect, and anger. Since they can't possibly create enthusiastic agreement from your spouse, you'll replace selfish demands with thoughtful requests and replace disrespectful judgments with respectful persuasion. And angry outbursts will simply be eliminated.

81

Does this all sound impossible to you? Maybe you're so used to making unilateral decisions that you've never really considered your spouse's feelings. But trust me, if you practice following the Policy of Joint Agreement, you'll get used to asking, "How do you feel about what I would like to do?" The policy forces you to be considerate and to understand each other's concerns. And that will bring you a giant step forward in your ability to negotiate.

At first, asking the question, "How would you feel?" will seem very strange to you and even humorous. That's to be expected—because your instincts and our culture don't encourage you to think in those terms. Yet that question is at the core of every fair negotiation in life, and you must force yourself to ask it until it becomes a habit.

But even after you've agreed to my rule, you may not be entirely familiar with what goes on between the question, "How do you feel about . . . ?" and the enthusiastic agreement. You may not have had much experience negotiating with each other.

So I suggest that you follow a step-by-step procedure that is used by almost all successful negotiators. Four simple guidelines will help you reach solutions that satisfy both of you and avoid dictators and anarchy. I call them the Four Guidelines for Successful Negotiation.

G u i d e l i n e 1:
Set ground rules to make negotiation pleasant and safe.

Most couples view marital negotiation as a trip to the torture chamber. That's because their efforts are usually fruitless, and they come away from the experience battered and bruised. Who wants to negotiate when you have nothing to look forward to but disappointment and pain?

So before you begin to negotiate, set some basic ground rules to make sure that you both enjoy the experience. Since you should negotiate as often as conflict arises, it should always be an enjoyable and safe experience for you both.

I suggest three basic ground rules:

Ground Rule 1: Try to be pleasant and cheerful throughout negotiations. It's fairly easy to start discussing an issue while in a good mood. But negotiations can open a can of worms and create negative emotional reactions. Your spouse may begin to feel uncomfortable about something you say. In fact, out of the clear blue, he or she may inform you that there will be no further discussion.

I know how upset and defensive couples can become when they first tell each other how they feel. So I tell them what I'm telling you—try to be as positive and cheerful as you can be, especially if your spouse says something that offends you.

Ground Rule 2: Put safety first—do not make demands, show disrespect, or become angry when you negotiate, even if your spouse does. Once the cat is out of the bag and you've told each other what you'd like to do or what's bothering you, you've entered one of the most dangerous phases of negotiation. If your feelings have been hurt, you're tempted to retaliate. Unless you make a special effort to resist demands, disrespect, and anger, you will revert to the Dictator Strategy, and your negotiation will turn into an argument. But if you can keep each other safe, you'll be able to use your intelligence to help you make the changes you both need.

Ground Rule 3: If you reach an impasse where you do not seem to be getting anywhere, or if one of you is starting to make demands, show disrespect, or become angry, stop negotiating and come back to the issue later. Just because you can't resolve a problem at a particular point in time doesn't mean you can't find an intelligent solution in the future. Don't let an impasse prevent you from giving yourself a chance to think about the issue. Let it incubate for a while, and you'll be amazed what your mind can do.

If your negotiation turns sour and one of you succumbs to the temptation of becoming a dictator (demands, disrespect, or anger), end the discussion by changing the subject to something more pleasant. After a brief pause, the offending spouse may apologize and wish to return to the subject that was so upsetting. But don't go back into the minefield until it has been swept clear of mines.

Guideline 2:

Identify the problem from both perspectives.

Once you've set ground rules that guarantee a safe and enjoyable discussion, you're ready to negotiate. But where do you begin? First, you must state the problem and then try to understand it from the perspectives of both you and your spouse.

Most couples go into marital negotiation without doing their homework. They don't fully understand the problem itself, nor do they understand each other's perspectives. In many cases, they aren't even sure what they really want.

Respect is key to success in this phase of negotiation. Once the problem has been identified and you hear each other's perspectives, it's extremely important to try to understand each other instead of trying to straighten each other out. Remember that your goal is enthusiastic agreement, and that can't happen if you reject each other's perspectives. The only way you'll reach an enthusiastic agreement is to come up with a solution that accommodates both perspectives as they are presented.

This point is so important that I will repeat it. *You will not solve your problem if you are disrespectful of each other's opinions.* In this stage of negotiation, you are to simply gather information that will help you understand what it will take to solve your problem. If you reject your spouse's opinions, you will be ignoring the facts. You should not talk over your spouse, try to talk your spouse out of his or her opinion, or even use mannerisms that could be interpreted as disrespectful (rolling eyes or sighing).

It's so much easier to negotiate the right way when your goal is enthusiastic agreement. It eliminates all the strategies that attempt to wear each other down with abuse. But when I take demands, disrespect, and anger away from some couples, they are left feeling naked. They feel helpless about resolving an issue without these tools. They're so used to being dictators that they simply don't know how to find win-win solutions to problems.

Is that how you and your spouse feel? If so, remember that with practice you'll become more comfortable approaching every conflict with the goal of mutual agreement. You'll learn to ask each other questions, not to embarrass each other but to gain a fuller understanding of what it would take to make each other happy. And when you think you have the information you need to consider win-win solutions, you're ready for the next step.

G u i d e l i n e 3:
Brainstorm with abandon.

You've set the ground rules. You've identified the problem and discovered each other's perspective. Now you're ready for the creative part—looking for mutually acceptable solutions. I know that can seem impossible if you and your spouse have drifted into incompatibility. But the climb back to compatibility has to start somewhere, and if you put your minds to it, you'll think of options that please you both.

Many well-intentioned but sadly misguided marital therapists recommend sacrifice in marriage. But a little thought should expose that approach as being terribly flawed. After all, whoever does the sacrificing would suffer, and what caring couple wants that for each other? They want mutual enjoyment with neither one suffering. It's only when we let our selfish instincts get the best of us that we expect our spouse to sacrifice for us.

You won't get very far if you allow yourself to think, "If she really loves me, she'll let me do this," or "He'll do this for me if he cares about me." Extraordinary care in marriage is not sacrificial care—it's **mutual** care. That means both spouses want the other to be happy, and neither spouse wants the other to be unhappy. If you care about your spouse, you should never expect, or even accept, sacrifice as a solution to a problem.

A subtle form of sacrifice is the "I'll let you do what you want this time if you let me do what I want next time" solution. For example, if you want to go out with your friends after work, leaving your spouse with the children, you may suggest that you take the children another night so that your spouse can go out with his or her friends. But this isn't a win-win situation: one of you ends up unhappy whenever the other is happy. And once you've made this agreement, it can easily turn into a habit that pulls you apart.

Win-lose solutions are common in marriage because most couples don't understand how to arrive at win-win solutions. Their concept of fairness is that both spouses should suffer equally. But isn't it better to find solutions in which neither spouse suffers? With a little creativity, you can make mutually acceptable decisions.

With sacrifice and suffering out of the question, you're ready to brainstorm. And quantity is often more important than quality. So let your minds run wild; go with any thought that might satisfy both of you simultaneously. When you let your creative juices flow, you are more likely to find the wisest solutions.

G u i d e l i n e 4:

Choose the solution that meets the conditions of the Policy of Joint Agreement— mutual and enthusiastic agreement.

After brainstorming, you'll have both good and bad solutions. Good solutions are those both you and your spouse consider desirable. Bad solutions, on the other hand, take the feelings of one spouse into account at the expense of the other. The best solution is the one that makes you and your spouse most enthusiastic.

Many problems are relatively easy to solve if you know you must take each other's feelings into account. That's because you become aware of what it will take to reach a mutual agreement. Instead of considering options that clearly are not in your spouse's best interest, you think of options you know would make both you and your spouse happy.

Consider the problem we mentioned above. You would like to go out with your friends after work, leaving your spouse with the children. Before you had agreed to the Policy of Joint Agreement, you may have simply called your spouse to say you'd be late or, worse yet, arrived home late without having called. But now you must come to an enthusiastic agreement prior to the event. It certainly restricts your freedom of choice, but on the other hand, it protects your spouse from your thoughtless behavior.

After having presented your case, you'd probably hear immediate objections. Your spouse might not appreciate your having fun while he or she is home battling the kids.

87

Help Needed

If you find it almost impossible to come to an enthusiastic agreement regarding certain behavior, you may be struggling with an addiction. Whether it's using drugs, alcohol, sex, gambling, or any other addictive behavior, you'll find that thoughtfulness is almost impossible to practice. The addiction is in complete control of your life, and you are helpless to protect your spouse from the suffering that it causes. If that's the case, you must sweep the addiction completely out of your life with professional treatment before you can negotiate in the way I've suggested.

"Besides," your spouse might mention, "our leisure activities should be with each other." In response, you might suggest that your spouse drop the children off with your parents (who *you* will call to make the arrangements) and join you.

If your spouse enthusiastically agrees, you are home free. Your parents take your children for a couple of hours, and your spouse joins you for the evening with your friends. Problem solved. In fact, if going out after work with friends becomes a regular event, you can plan ahead for it by arranging the childcare in advance!

Of course, other problems can be more difficult to solve, involving many steps. But with some trial and error, you should eventually find a mutually agreeable solution.

Practice Makes Perfect

If you follow the four guidelines I've suggested, negotiation can be an enjoyable way to learn about each other. And when you reach a solution that makes you both happy, you'll make substantial deposits into each other's Love Banks. In the end, the Policy of Joint Agreement not only helps you become a great negotiator, it also protects your love for each other.

As you've been reading my guidelines for successful negotiation, you may be wondering if you have what it

Getting in Shape to Negotiate

I suggest this exercise to build the habits of successful negotiation.

Go to a grocery store together without your children, and for about fifteen minutes find items for your cart that you would both be enthusiastic about buying. This shopping is purely for practice, so you don't need to actually purchase any of the items in your cart when you're finished. I chose grocery shopping so you will have a chance to practice making win-win decisions on an issue that has no real emotional impact for either of you. That way, you can avoid the unpleasant reactions that accompany the real conflicts you may be having.

If one of you wants an item that the other is not enthusiastic about buying, negotiate to try to create enthusiasm. But avoid making bargains that let you have one item that your spouse doesn't like in exchange for your spouse having an item you don't like. Make sure every item that goes in the cart is chosen with an enthusiastic agreement. The very act of asking each other how you feel regarding each item in question, and holding off on making a decision until you have agreement, is an extremely important habit to learn if you want to create a mutually enjoyable lifestyle.

It's perfectly okay to accept an item on a trial basis. "Try it, you'll like it" is a legitimate negotiating strategy. If your spouse is willing to try the item, take it home and taste it. If it's acceptable, add it to your cart the next time you practice. If not, leave it on the shelf.

Repeat this exercise on several occasions until you can fill your cart with groceries in the fifteen minutes you have scheduled. Each time you begin, you can go right to the items that you've already agreed to purchase, put them in your cart, and negotiate about new items. A full cart symbolizes a complete lifestyle with all of its component parts benefiting both of you.

When you think you've gotten the hang of coming to an enthusiastic agreement about groceries, tackle some real conflicts you've been unable to resolve. You'll probably be amazed at how quickly the Policy of Joint Agreement takes root.

takes to build a lifetime of love. It may just seem like too much to remember. But thankfully, once you establish the habit of negotiating with each other, it will be easy to run through the steps whenever there is a problem to solve. It's like learning to type. At first it seems impossible, but with practice, it becomes almost instinctive.

If you and your spouse have found yourselves acting more like dictators than sweethearts, it may seem overwhelming to switch to successful negotiations. But the guidelines can be implemented almost effortlessly if you practice them. Any behavior can seem automatic when repeated often enough.

A Policy That Promotes Care

The Policy of Joint Agreement promotes a total lifestyle of extraordinary care in which every aspect of your life is for your mutual benefit. It's a lifestyle you can both enjoy. And that's exactly what you'll eventually have if you make all of your decisions with mutual agreement.

When you wake up each morning, both of you will look forward to the way the day is planned. You will enjoy raising your children, the way you spend your money, the friends you have chosen, your careers, and everything else that forms your way of life. But if you don't make your decisions with mutual agreement, you will not only find your life to be very stressful and plagued with problems, but you will also feel uncared for and unloved.

A successful marriage requires extraordinary care. You expect it when you marry, and you will find yourselves very disillusioned if you don't have it after marriage. So spare yourself a very disappointing marriage by giving each other the extraordinary care you promised. And an essential way to provide that care is to follow the Policy of Joint Agreement.

6

Our Culture and Care Don't Mix

Overcoming Cultural Obstacles to Extraordinary Care

We've just spent the past four chapters looking at how important it is to provide extraordinary care in marriage. It's the first essential ingredient for a traditional marriage, and anyone can learn to provide it. But it's not easy. There are internal forces that work against extraordinary care—our instincts make it seem unnatural to invest the effort it takes to provide such care to our spouse. And there are also external forces—the voices of our culture make it seem completely unreasonable as well. So before we move on to the second essential ingredient for a traditional marriage, let's take a closer look at those cultural influences, and what we can do to resist them.

My wife, Joyce, and I can remember facing some of those cultural influences already in the 1960s when we were first married. At that time a growing number of educated women were angry at what they considered lost opportunities caused by marriage. They felt that women who had the same ability as men to rise to the top of economic and political power were being overlooked because of the roles that culture, and men, had placed on them.

But there was more. Many less educated women felt trapped in their marriages. They felt stuck in the role of wife and mother—dependent upon their husbands for their financial security and for their happiness. Some men took advantage of that dependence. Instead of providing security, they physically abused their wives. Instead of providing happiness, they believed that financial support was all that should be required of them—and they ignored their wife's other emotional needs.

The growing dissatisfaction of married women in the 1950s and early '60s was reflected in books and articles. In 1965 *Redbook* magazine asked readers who had never published a magazine article to submit entries entitled, "Why Young Mothers Feel Trapped." The magazine promised to publish the best in an upcoming issue. But when they received over fifty thousand articles, they decided to select thirty-two and publish them in book form. The passion expressed in those articles together with the range of ways the women felt trapped was a predictor of things to come.[1]

Yet overall, marriage wasn't really all that bad for most women at that time. In fact, studies of marital satisfaction found that most wives were happily married. There were very few divorces in those days—only about one in ten marriages ended in divorce. So while there may have been a growing number of women who were unhappy with marriage, the vast majority were satisfied with the arrangement. And Joyce was among them. She stayed home to raise our children while I worked to support our family. She would not have had it any other way because we both provided extraordinary care for each other.

But eventually those women who felt trapped in marriage grew to a critical mass and began to receive unprecedented attention. Books and articles were written to convince women that the roles they had been playing as wife and mother not only cheated them out of valuable opportunities but also blocked their escape from abusive husbands. Led by feminists, many women decided to abandon those roles and create for themselves a new way of life. Instead of providing extraordinary care for their husbands, they began to ignore them and provided extraordinary care for themselves.

As one might expect, the rate of divorce skyrocketed in response. It jumped from about 10 percent in the 1950s to about 50 percent in the 1980s. After peaking in 1981, the divorce rate has settled in at about 43 percent. While that number is still very high, those who remain married are not necessarily satisfied. In fact, an additional 20 percent are permanently separated by the time they die. And even those who remain together for life are not always happy—about half of them are simply trying to put up with each other. I estimate that only about one marriage in five (20 percent) is like the one that Joyce and I have created.

What Went Wrong?

It isn't the institution of marriage itself that leads to so much unhappiness. It's the failure of husbands and wives to provide each other the extraordinary care that they expected at the time of their wedding. So you'd think that extraordinary care in marriage would be taught in schools and churches. It's that important. But instead, we're being taught just the opposite. The secular and religious values of our culture actually tend to discourage us from providing the kind of care that is needed for a happy marriage.

Cultural Obstacle 1: We're encouraged to neglect each other's needs, instead of trying to meet them.

As I mentioned in chapter 3, there are many who don't believe that we can or should try to make each other happy in marriage. At weddings, I often hear ministers admonish couples not to expect their needs to be met by each other. Instead, say these ministers, each spouse should look to themselves or God to meet their needs. That advice sets couples on a very dangerous course in life because they are both led to believe that they should not try to make each other happy. If they follow that advice, it isn't long before their romantic relationship, which was created precisely because they *did* make each other happy, becomes a distant memory.

What could these ministers be thinking? A husband and wife *must* meet each other's emotional needs if they expect to remain in love with each other. What could have possibly convinced such ministers otherwise? Their own less-than-happy marriages perhaps? After all, the marriages of ministers aren't much better than those of their congregation. So if only about one in five of their marriages is actually a happy marriage, that might explain their misguided advice. It takes someone with a great marriage to know how important it is to meet emotional needs, and there are many fewer of those people around these days.

But the clergy are not the only source of discouragement. The codependency movement has also contributed to the problem. What began as an important part of helping addicts overcome their addiction has become an absolute marriage wrecker. Advocates of this movement encourage couples to avoid trying to make their

94

spouses happy, calling such an effort *codependency* (see my article, "Why the Codependency Movement is Ruining Marriages," in the articles section of the website www.marriagebuilders .com).

I've been shocked at how many addicts end up divorced after they become sober. And much of the blame, I'm afraid, lies at the feet of those who discourage addicts' spouses from trying to please them after their recovery, arguing that such behavior is codependent.

When that same message reaches spouses who have never struggled with addiction, it has the same outcome. They also divorce. The message that we cannot, or should not, try to make each other happy in marriage has a devastating effect if people take it seriously.

Some of our cultural practices also undermine the willingness and ability of couples to meet each other's needs. Dual careers are a cultural obstacle to meeting needs because they create acute scheduling problems. The rise in after-school sporting activities for parents and children to attend does the same thing. Mind you, a dual career and after-school sports do not prevent a couple from meeting each other's emotional needs. But they do make it much more difficult to achieve.

It's usually possible for even the busiest of couples to fit everything that's important into their schedules if they plan carefully enough. That's because most people

> ## Finding Fifteen Hours
>
> When I first challenge couples to schedule fifteen hours each week for the exclusive purpose of meeting each other's intimate emotional needs, most of them don't believe it's possible. They don't think they have an extra fifteen hours. But when it's finally scheduled, they usually discover that it's not only possible, but it's essential to their marriage. And they're also able to accomplish everything else that's important to them. The time was there all along, but it was being spent in ways that were far less important.

waste quite a bit of time when their lives are unscheduled. So I encourage you to live scheduled lives. That way you'll prioritize your time to achieve everything that's important in life—including the meeting of each other's needs.

There are some decisions, however—particularly certain vocational decisions—that force couples into a life of neglect in spite of careful planning. Consider a career in the military, for example. Couples who are apart for months or even years at a time have no opportunity to meet each other's intimate emotional needs on a regular basis. Is it any wonder that these couples divorce at a very high rate? The same is true of those working as airline pilots or flight attendants who are gone for several days at a time. They also have a high rate of divorce. In fact, any career that prevents a husband and wife from being together almost every night is associated with a much higher than average incidence of divorce.

Split shifts have the same disastrous effect on marriage. When one spouse works one shift while the other works another, they *can* save money on childcare. But what they save in money, they lose in Love Bank deposits. These marriages are notoriously unhappy because a split shift prevents them from meeting each other's intimate emotional needs. I've found that when I can convince couples to change their careers or work the same shift so they can have easier and more frequent access to each other, their marriages flourish. And they also find that with a great marriage, their careers flourish as well.

The bottom line is that extraordinary care begins with meeting important emotional needs. Spouses who understand that fact don't let anything get between them, and they become experts at making each other happy. Those who do not understand it soon find themselves very disillusioned with marriage.

Cultural Obstacle 2: We are encouraged to ignore each other's complaints instead of trying to respond to them.

When my wife, Joyce, tells me that I'm doing something that's bothering her, how should I respond? Many marital therapists would tell me that Joyce is making a mistake by criticizing me and that I should ignore her criticism. Then they would turn to Joyce and tell her that nothing I do short of physical or verbal abuse should make her unhappy—that she's *choosing* to let me bother her. If she doesn't like something I'm doing, they suggest that we are too enmeshed in each other's lives and should spend more time apart. They recommend she create emotional barriers to protect her from that behavior. And the result, of course, is the elimination of our romantic relationship because intimacy, and the emotional vulnerability it creates, is essential if we are to be in love with each other.

When I counsel husbands with complaining wives (or vice versa), I explain that when their spouse stops complaining, they can kiss their romantic relationship good-bye. Complaints are common in a romantic relationship because partners are affected by each other much more intensely. When spouses complain, it's partly due to their emotionally close proximity, and the correct response to such a complaint is to apologize and try to be more thoughtful.

Our laws and culture have correctly targeted abuse and control in marriage as something that should not be tolerated. In fact, the incidence of physical abuse has been in steady decline for the past twenty years. Today there is little debate about the issue, and abusive spouses seem to be getting the message.

But while our culture makes it clear that abuse and control is the wrong way to solve marital conflicts, it offers little help in pointing couples in the right direction. Selfish demands, disrespectful judgments, and angry outbursts are all seen as terribly inappropriate, and yet few couples are encouraged to solve their problems the right way—by finding solutions that take the interests of both spouses into account simultaneously. They are encouraged to respect each other's opinions but discouraged from coming to a mutually enthusiastic agreement. So when conflicts arise, they don't know how to resolve them.

Dishonesty is another Love Buster that seems to be encouraged by our culture. Marital therapists often suggest that a little dishonesty is essential to our identity and self-esteem. Moreover, many feel that privacy is far more important than honesty and that, even in marriage, no one should feel obligated to reveal what they do secretly.

Even annoying habits are often viewed as part of our identity. If you find your spouse to be annoying, therapists suggest that you should learn to be more tolerant, and be willing to accept diversity. So instead of making ourselves more pleasant to be around, we're told to expect others to be more tolerant of our thoughtlessness. Don't buy into that message. It will destroy your marriage if you do.

Cultural Obstacle 3: We are encouraged to create a self-centered lifestyle instead of one that's mutually enjoyable.

The first two parts of my definition of extraordinary care in marriage are somewhat intuitive—try to make each other happy and avoid making each other unhappy. It's just common sense. In spite of cultural forces that lobby against these crucial goals of marriage, most people would agree with me that marriage isn't worth much if spouses don't try to make each other happy and avoid making each other unhappy.

But the third part—creating a mutually enjoyable lifestyle—is just as important as the first two, yet it's not nearly as intuitive. While most people see the value of trying to meet emotional needs in marriage, and also of trying to protect their spouse from some of their more unpleasant predispositions, some of their lifestyle choices seem too personal for compromise.

"Why should my spouse determine my career, my hobbies, my church, and even my car?" they argue. "They're reflections of who I am." It's that kind of thinking that often prompts couples to go their separate ways within marriage—each living their own life and coming together only when convenient.

As I was reading *Readers Digest* recently, I found an article entitled, "The Science of a Happy Marriage," by Michael Gurian.[2] The subtitle of this article was, "By nature, men and women aren't made for each other. How to outsmart our DNA and live happily ever after." Since I was completely unaware of any DNA research that suggested that men and women were not made for each other, I looked for references in the article to "scientific" evidence for the author's claims. Of course, there were none.

Michael Gurian is a social philosopher who has written numerous books on the differences between men and women. I'm in agreement with his basic thesis that men and women are different. In fact, I've built my reputation on that fact. I identified some of those differences at a time when feminists wanted us to believe that there were none. When I taught neurophysiology in college, I demonstrated that difference to my students by showing them an adult male brain and an adult female brain. They look very different, and they are very different—male brains are simply not made the same as female brains.

Men and women really are profoundly different—physiologically, neurologically, and emotionally—and those differences must be taken into account in creating a great marriage. If they're ignored, those differences can cause overwhelming problems.

The Five Stages of [Failed] Marriage

Failed marriages are so common these days that some people think that they define marriage. As I mentioned earlier, I estimate that only one marriage in five meets my standards of a successful marriage—one that is happy and romantic throughout life. Many of today's marriage commentators don't know much about those successful marriages—they know more about failed marriages because there are so many more of them. And those are the ones they use to draw their conclusions.

The five stages of marriage that Michael Gurian describes are (1) romance, (2) disillusionment, (3) power struggle, (4) awakening, and finally, (5) long-term marriage. Sadly, he's not alone in his analysis. There are many others who have offered roughly the same list of marital stages. Locke Rush,[3] for example, names the five stages as (1) romance, (2) disillusionment, (3) misery, (4) enlightenment, and (5) love—slightly different names for the same stages.

What Gurian and others are describing as the final and most desirable stage, however, is not "long-term marriage" or "love." They're describing those who have failed marriages but have decided not to divorce. The marriages they describe begin with romance, as most marriages do, but when they fail to provide extraordinary care, they proceed to disillusionment, followed by a power struggle. At that point they feel they have one of two choices: either divorce or come to the conclusion that a mature marital relationship is not romantic. They "awaken" to the belief that romance is possible only in the beginning of a relationship, and if they want a long-term marriage they must give up hope for a romantic marriage. When that happens, according to Gurian and others, the couple is able to settle into a long-term marriage.

Gurian maintains that when the

But Gurian draws a conclusion that is not supported by a shred of scientific evidence. He thinks that because men and women are different, we are somehow not made for each other. How could he have come to that conclusion? We sure look like we're made for each other!

I'm not in a position to know, but it could be his per-most mature and successful stage of marriage is reached, a husband and wife develop different sets of friends, create separate hobbies or sporting activities, and, in general, create totally separate lives. They experience a realization that they can remain married only if they have as little to do with each other as possible.

To put it another way, Gurian believes that couples go through an irrational struggle to blend the lives of a man and woman. They do that because a romantic relationship requires it. But after they become exhausted trying to achieve the impossible, both spouses are awakened to find themselves hopelessly different, and they stop trying to blend their lives—they give up on romance.

Most of those who read Gurian's article will be able to relate to his five stages of marriage. In fact, as I mentioned earlier, about 80 percent of marriages either divorce after reaching the third stage of marriage or stick it out for the sake of their children or for some other reason.

And they find that an independent lifestyle helps them survive each other. But these are the failed marriages.

Gurian concludes, "There's tremendous value in knowing that your feelings toward one another are likely to change over time and that change is normal."[4] In other words, you will fall out of love with each other, and when you do, it's the way nature intended things to be. Don't fight the inevitable.

Are Gurian's five stages of marriage really inevitable? Do all of us who have been married for a while agree that we've passed through these stages?

Well, Joyce and I have been married for forty-two years, and so far we have only experienced the "romance" stage. We haven't yet come to the disillusionment or power struggle stages. And I'd stake my life on the claim that we never will as long as we keep giving each other extraordinary care.

sonal experience that has led him astray. Just as some of the most strident feminists try to ruin the entire institution of marriage because of their own personal failures, I've found that many social theorists question the possibility of men and women ever forming a lasting romantic bond because they've never done it themselves. If he had expe-

101

rienced the same great marital relationship that Joyce and I have together, I doubt he would have concluded that men and women are not made for each other.

Joyce and I have done something that I doubt Gurian and others ever really achieved or even attempted. We have provided each other extraordinary care from the first year of our marriage right up to the present. We meet each other's emotional needs, and we protect each other from our destructive instincts. But we also do something else—we blend our lives together—something Gurian thinks is impossible for a man and woman to do. Instead of having separate friends, hobbies, and sporting activities, we have the same friends, hobbies, and sporting activities. In fact, all of our lifestyle choices are a blending of our interests and feelings. Before either of us makes a decision, we first check with the other to be sure that it's acceptable. We are each other's best friend and have created compatibility. We've been successful in establishing a blended lifestyle.

At this point most feminists might argue that what I call "blending" they would call "enslavement." But I challenge any of them to talk with Joyce. All those who know her well are assured that she is not, never has been, and never will be enslaved by me or anyone else. The fact that our lives are integrated does not mean that either of us has enslaved the other. It means we're partners with equal power and equal rights in our relationship.

Others may argue that Joyce and I were born to be more compatible than most men and women. But again, anyone who knows us well would say that Joyce and I are very different from each other. She is characteristically feminine in her interests and instincts, and I am characteristically masculine in my interests and instincts. We have *created* compatibility—we certainly weren't born with it.

Granted, it's more difficult for a man and woman to create a blended lifestyle than it is to create independent lifestyles. But that doesn't mean we're not made for each other. When a man and woman create interdependence, they find such incredible fulfillment that it proves what married couples have known for thousands of years—they fit perfectly.

The very word, *marriage*, suggests the blending of something. And in the case of traditional marriage, it's the blending of two lives. So this third part of extraordinary care focuses attention on the central meaning of marriage—two people joining together to become partners in life. It's not only possible, but it's essential in creating a successful marriage. And a successful marriage is a romantic marriage.

Cultural Obstacle 4: We are led to believe that permanent romance in marriage isn't possible.

Having spent most of my professional career helping married couples survive infidelity, I know quite a bit about romantic relationships. Here's a letter I received recently from an unfaithful husband who wants to end his affair.[5]

Dear Dr. Harley,

I know I should end my relationship with Cathy, but my feelings are so strong. She means a lot to me, and we fit each other like a hand and glove. How do I walk away from someone who is my soulmate. We get along better than anyone I've ever known, and I am very attracted to her physically and also to her personality. I have not spoken to her for four days. How long will this pain last?

Brian

Brian is describing what it feels like to be in a romantic relationship, but he's in love with the wrong person. It's his wife he should be talking about, not Cathy. Those who think a romantic relationship cannot be sustained in marriage would tell Brian that he has a choice—either end all hope of romantic relationship by leaving Cathy and going back to his wife, or leave his wife and enjoy his romantic relationship. But I give Brian a third choice—have a romantic relationship with your wife. In other words, he can feel toward his wife the way he feels toward Cathy. And I've helped thousands of couples achieve that objective over the past thirty-five years. I do it by showing them how to give each other the extraordinary care that they should have been providing each other all along.

The Path of Care and Consideration

In the 1960s and '70s the rate of divorce reached unprecedented levels partly because spouses were not encouraged to give each other extraordinary care in marriage. They were not encouraged to meet each other's emotional needs, and they were not encouraged to avoid Love Busters. But what was most obvious was that they were not encouraged to make lifestyle decisions with each other in mind. In fact, they were encouraged to do the opposite—to make lifestyle decisions that would not necessarily be approved by their spouse.

They regarded the care that their parents gave each other as being far too restrictive. Even though most of their parents were happy with the way they lived, they felt that such extraordinary care limited their potential in life. They felt that their personal potential would be sacrificed if they let a spouse's feelings influence their goals in life.

But thirty years later, most of the children of that generation don't even know what extraordinary care in marriage looks like. Their divorced parents didn't provide each other the kind of care that their grandparents provided each other. As a result they have no example to follow, even when they want to do so.

Many of those planning to marry don't want to make the same mistakes their parents made. They have seen firsthand the misery of a bad marriage and the tragedy of divorce. They're not at all convinced that the me-first philosophy of their parents is right for them. But without an example of extraordinary care, they don't know how to create the kind of marriage that their grandparents enjoyed.

If your parents were divorced, you may be thinking that the level of extraordinary care I propose is much too difficult for any human being to deliver. Making someone happy by meeting important emotional needs and avoiding someone's unhappiness by controlling our basic predispositions is difficult enough. But making every decision with someone else in mind is, well, unrealistic.

Yet that's precisely what a husband and wife do for each other in good marriages. Granted, good marriages that remain good throughout life are hard to find these days. But those who have them are not exceptional people. They are average people who have chosen a path of care and consideration rather than a path of self-centeredness. And that's what it takes to create an exceptional marriage.

I'm not describing some unachievable ideal in marriage. I'm describing what my own parents did for each other and what my wife, Joyce, and I do for each other. And we do it with ease. It may seem difficult if you've never witnessed extraordinary care or if you've never practiced it. But once you learn how to provide it for each other, your life will be much easier than it has been—not more difficult. A good marriage isn't hard to achieve; it's a bad marriage that is too much work.

PART 2

"FORSAKING ALL OTHERS"

Romantic Exclusivity

7

One of Life's Most Devastating Experiences

The Curse of Infidelity

Al just didn't seem to be himself. He didn't sleep well, he was easily distracted, and he was very irritable, particularly when Judy, his wife of seventeen years, was around.

"What's going on?" Judy asked one day.

"Going on?" he replied. "What do you mean?"

"You seem to be upset about something."

It took a minute for Al to answer. Finally, he said, "Oh, it's nothing," and left the room.

Judy had never been much of a snoop, but Al's behavior, coupled with that very unsatisfactory response, worried her. So while Al was out on an errand, she went through his desk, rifling through all his drawers.

Finding nothing of interest there, she went to his computer and opened his email folder, checking every file. Under the category "Snow Blower," she hit pay dirt. Al had been carrying on an email romance with Alice, someone he met on the Internet who lived nearby. He had saved all of the letters they had written to each other in a file that would seem innocent.

Through her tears, Judy read every letter, from the first, written about ten months earlier, to the last, which had been written that very morning. It had started as a simple email friendship, with each of them passing on personal interests and observations—nothing very alarming. But as time passed, the letters became much more intimate in tone.

Alice was the first to express her feelings toward Al, and he dutifully reminded her that he was a married man with three children. But it wasn't long before he admitted to her that his feelings were changing and that he wanted to meet her. From that point on the email letters reflected how much fun they had whenever they were together and how right they were for each other. They even alluded to occasional sexual encounters.

Judy was devastated. How could Al have done this to her? Why would he have done it? Her mind was racing as she hoped it would turn out to be nothing more than a bad dream. But if it were not a dream, how should she respond? Should she beg him to stay with her? Should she leave him? She could feel her heart beating faster and faster as she thought of losing the man she loved. But if she stayed with him, could she ever trust him again?

The Curse of Infidelity

Infidelity has risen to epidemic proportions in America. But it's very difficult to get accurate information about this curse to traditional marriage. Producers of popular television shows for each of the major networks have asked me to find couples willing to tell their story of infidelity. Since I've helped literally thousands of these couples recover from the devastation that it causes, you'd think that at least one of them would be willing to come forward. But over the past ten years not one couple has volunteered. They are all too ashamed.

A recent survey by the National Opinion Research Center (University of Chicago) found that 25 percent of men and 17 percent of women admitted to being unfaithful.[1] Those findings are shocking enough when you consider the suffering that infidelity causes. But I'm convinced that the real numbers are much larger.

In our own study of the prevalence of infidelity, we asked people that we knew had been unfaithful the following question: "If you were asked in an anonymous survey if you or your spouse had ever had an affair, would you admit it?" Can you guess how it turned out? Forty-seven percent of the men and 58 percent of the women answered with an emphatic "no!"

The spouses of those I questioned already knew about their affair, so they had nothing to hide from them. And many of those surveyed were not the ones who were unfaithful—it was their spouses who cheated. But only 53 percent of the men and only 42 percent of women we interviewed were willing to admit it in a survey. So if 25 percent of men and 17 percent of women surveyed *admit* to having an affair but only 53 percent of men and only 42 percent of women who have actually *had* an affair or whose spouse had an affair will admit to it, what would be the true percentage of spouses who have had affairs? When you adjust the percentages to account for the percent of respondents who weren't willing to admit their infidelity, you come up with a new estimate of about

Not a Happy Ending

If Al had ended his affair with Alice the day he was discovered and had put as much effort into rebuilding his relationship with Judy as he had invested in his relationship with Alice, slowly but surely, Judy's nightmare would have ended.

But affairs do not usually end once they are discovered, and Al's affair was no exception. With Judy present, he called Alice the next day to announce the end of their relationship. Although she agreed on the telephone to abide by his decision and avoid contacting him in the future, Alice wrote him an email at work that very day. Al responded, and their relationship continued—this time with more effort to avoid detection.

Since Judy no longer trusted Al, she suspected that he might continue his affair. So she kept a very close eye on his comings and goings. And it wasn't long before she caught him in a parking lot, embracing Alice.

Judy walked up to the car and knocked on the window, surprising them both. Al immediately locked the door, and that threw Judy into an uncontrollable rage. She started screaming at him to get out of the car, but instead, he drove away, taking Alice with him. After finally returning home, he found Judy and his children gone. They had moved in with her parents. And within a year, they were divorced.

Al's relationship with Alice continued for a few months, but his constant struggle with guilt, and his efforts to try to win Judy back, made him a terrible lover. So by the time of their divorce, Al had lost both Judy and Alice.

Judy was devastated, the children were devastated, and even Al was devastated. It isn't at all what he thought it would be—a harmless game of romance played on the Internet. Instead, it turned out to be an overdose of pain and suffering for those he cared for most.

47 percent of men and about 40 percent of women who have had affairs.

And this estimate is based on unfaithful spouses who have been discovered! What about those whose spouse does not yet know about the affair? If you had an affair and your spouse didn't know about it, would you admit it to someone doing a survey? It could be your suspicious spouse trying to trick you! It's safe to assume that very few of these people would admit to an affair.

So is everyone having an affair? Well, I wouldn't go quite that far. I haven't had an affair, and I'm sure that there are many like me who go through life having figured out how to avoid them. But I'm also sure that the percentage is much higher than 25 percent. My best estimate based on my years of experience helping married couples is that it's probably higher than 60 percent—even for women.

That's a frightening statistic when you consider the suffering affairs cause. And when infidelity is discovered (as it frequently is, given today's advances in technology), it has a devastating affect on a marriage. In fact, my counseling experience and examination of failed marriages leads me to name infidelity as the number one cause of divorce in America.

Side Effect: Suffering

Infidelity is not only a major cause of divorce, it's also one of the major causes of human suffering, especially among women. Divorce is emotionally destructive to the betrayed spouse and children—and to the unfaithful spouse and the lover. Both active players and innocent bystanders in this tragic human drama soon find out that infidelity creates personal disaster for them.

Over my thirty-five years as a clinical psychologist treating thousands of patients, I have seen just about all of the ways that people can hurt each other. And I've found infidelity to be one of the most emotionally devastating ways. Women I've counseled who have experienced both rape and their husband's infidelity have consistently agreed that their husband's affair was far more painful to them and took much longer to overcome emotionally than their rape.

Women who were molested during their childhood have given me similar reports. Their husband's affair was more emotionally devastating to them than the sexual abuse they suffered as children. A woman whose house was destroyed by fire admitted to me that her husband's affair created more lasting trauma for her than the fire's destruction. And women who were physically abused by husbands who were also unfaithful have also consistently reported more emotional damage from the affair than from the physical abuse.

For those women who have been raped, sexually abused as children, or physically abused, and have not experienced the tragedy of an affair, these testimonials might be very difficult to believe. But we have interviewed scores of women who had experienced these tragedies and many others along with infidelity, and the reports are always the same. An affair is one of life's most devastating experiences.

But despite this extreme suffering, there are couples who have asked me to help them restore their marriage even after this tragic experience. And I have become an expert in helping couples achieve that objective.

Laws to Prevent Infidelity

I've found that the first step every couple must take if they want to recover from infidelity is to permanently end the affair. The unfaithful spouse and the lover should never see or talk to each other again. But how can you do that when an affair is so addictive?

In the early 1970s, one of the tools that I found quite useful for helping spouses end affairs was the threat of a civil lawsuit against the spouse's lover. Such a suit could be filed for seduction (attempting to engage a married person in a romantic relationship), criminal conversation (having sexual intercourse with a married person), and alienation of affections (having an affair with a married person). With such a lawsuit, the lover of the unfaithful spouse could be held liable for damages due to efforts to draw the unfaithful spouse from his or her marital obligations. The lover could be single or married. If the lover were married, it was technically possible for both betrayed spouses to sue. But in most cases, I found the threat of such a lawsuit was sufficient to end the affair, especially when the lover was an owner or manager of a business where the unfaithful spouse worked.

> **Seduction**
>
> Attempting to engage a married person in a romantic relationship
>
> **Criminal Conversation**
>
> Having sexual intercourse with a married person
>
> **Alienation of Affections**
>
> Having an affair with a married person

The threat of a lawsuit not only helped me end affairs, but in many of the cases I witnessed, it also nipped them in the bud. Whenever I would counsel an unhappy spouse who was considering an affair, the very mention of civil laws against such behavior and penalties for their violation was sufficient to encourage the spouse to find an alternative solution—straightening out his or her marriage.

But in 1978 the Minnesota Legislature passed a law prohibiting civil lawsuits for seduction, criminal conversations, and alienation of affections. This abandonment of laws to protect innocent people and marriages granted impunity to anyone who used seduction and infidelity to torment others or to try to break up a family. What's more, justification for abandoning those laws seemed to encourage infidelity—because infidelity was viewed as

A Double Standard

While laws protecting spouses against emotional suffering caused by infidelity were being revoked, other laws covering emotional suffering for other causes were actually expanded. For example, civil damages for the emotional suffering from rape or even an automobile accident can now easily run into millions of dollars.

Only the suffering of a betrayed spouse was eliminated from consideration by law. The new law provided protection to the perpetrators of the incredible suffering that infidelity causes and took protection away from their victims by removing the right to appeal to the courts for redress of a particularly devastating attack.

too trivial an offense to be worth the court's time. This legalization of infidelity has greatly weakened the family because now spouses and children no longer have any legal protection from it's devastating consequences.

As I've already mentioned, I've found that infidelity is one of the most emotionally damaging experiences a betrayed spouse can face in life. As a clinical psychologist, I have observed the emotional and physical damage it causes and have witnessed how difficult it is to treat effectively. It's not a trivial matter—it tears families apart and is one of the most serious social problems we face in our society. For the courts to ignore it is to turn a blind eye to one of the greatest threats to families and one of the greatest causes of emotional trauma.

At the very least, the law legalizing alienation of affections should be rescinded. But we need more than a simple reenactment of the old laws against seduction, criminal conversation, and alienation of affections. We need a new law that draws special attention to crimes committed by those who threaten the family. Such laws would make it clear to the public that as a society, we understand the suffering that infidelity causes and we want to help prevent such destructive behavior.

The Case for Revocation of the Law

According to the 1978 Minnesota law, action was taken because the old laws against infidelity were "subject to grave abuses, have caused intimidation and harassment to innocent persons, and have resulted in the perpetration of frauds." Yet there was absolutely no evidence that there were any abuses. No cases were presented to illustrate the point, and no "victims" of such lawsuits ever came forward to describe how they were intimidated, were harassed, or were the targets of fraud. People simply assumed that there must be such cases in existence, because other states had used the same argument to rescind similar laws.

Of course, there is potential for intimidation and harassment in every law, but why single out infidelity as being particularly vulnerable? Careful analysis demonstrates quite convincingly that such lawsuits were no more subject to abuse than any other laws. And we have other laws in place that provide protection from frivolous lawsuits in such cases.

William R. Corbett, professor of law at the Paul M. Hebert Law Center of Louisiana State University, has written the most well-researched and persuasive argument on this subject that I have seen. He has examined every objection that has ever been proposed to the laws concerning seduction, criminal conversation, and alienation of affections. In addition to the objection of intimidation and harassment used in Minnesota, he found arguments concerning property issues, claiming that the laws do not necessarily deter extramarital relations, citing the problem of trying to legislate morality, referring to the intangible and speculative nature of damages, blaming the marriage itself to some extent, alleging the possibility of revenge issues, and contending that seduction is protected by our freedom of speech.

117

Considering every possible argument, Corbett demonstrates very convincingly that the laws against seduction, criminal conversation, and alienation of affections do not differ from other laws that we enthusiastically support. He argues that the reason these laws have been challenged has less to do with their uselessness than with their original ties to the feminist movement in America. When first conceived, feminists felt that women were exclusively the targets of such laws and that the laws tended to enslave them. But today, even feminists recognize that women are the most likely victims of adultery. They are the ones who report suffering most.[2]

Corbett also introduces an important problem: the original laws did not adequately prevent adultery or save marriages. While eliminating them entirely made matters worse, he argues that they should not return as they originally appeared. Instead, they should return with a greater emphasis on the purpose of the laws—stopping infidelity and preserving marriages. In fact, he suggests that a new statute be drafted that would be entitled Intentional Interference with Marriage. Though he never went so far as to actually draft such a law, Corbett does provide us some guidance.

Intentional Interference with Marriage

Before we can draft any new law, we need to look back at the terms used in the old laws: *seduction, alienation of affections*, and *criminal conversations*. Corbett believes that laws against seduction, in the widest possible use of the term, could be seen to violate first amendment rights of free speech. For example, to advise or encourage someone to consider divorcing his or her spouse might be considered a form of seduction. But a mother should be able to encourage her daughter to divorce her abusive son-in-law without fear of a lawsuit. Likewise, a coun-selor should be able to suggest to a client that he or she consider divorce as a possible action.

Where seduction crosses the line is if it's part of an effort to replace a person's spouse in a romantic relation-ship, especially if sex is involved. So a new law would need to clarify the meaning of *seduction*. We already have sexual harassment laws to protect an individual from unwanted advances. But at present, the law does not protect the spouse. If a new law also granted a spouse protection, it would be easier to prosecute anyone making a sexual advance that is unwanted by either the person or that person's spouse. That way, those with a position of authority (lawyers, ministers, bosses, etc.), who might prevent someone from reporting or even objecting to the incident through intimidation, could be sued by a spouse who is not intimidated.

Corbett also finds problems with the traditional defi-nition of *alienation of affections*. In many court cases, damages hung on the issue of whether there were any *affections* in the first place. An unfaithful spouse would merely argue that affections had been missing for years, and so there was nothing to alienate. Yet in spite of that problem, there were not many judges or juries who gave ground on the intent of the law—that a married couple should be protected from outside interference so they would have an opportunity to regain their affection for each other.

Corbett has absolutely no problem with a law against *criminal conversation* (sexual intercourse) except for its name. It should be called *sexual acts* and would include anything that is intended to arouse sexual feelings, includ-ing activities such as oral sex.

The underlying purpose and scope of the new law should make it clear that adultery is wrong and that it is punishable. To the extent that alienation of affections and criminal conversations could be written to make that point clear, it would become a valuable law.

A New Law

So what do I recommend? Ultimately, I would like to see new laws written to help prevent adultery and save marriages. Such laws would send the message that infidelity is *not* a trivial matter and that those who suffer from it have the right to have their grievances addressed in a court of law and to demand damages for the suffering they have sustained.

Throughout human history, and in almost all cultures, infidelity has been seen as incredibly destructive to society and has been severely punished. Yet in most states today we have no criminal laws that forbid this behavior.

I've written this book in part to draw attention to the *crime* of infidelity and its unspeakable consequences to our families and to our society in general. But I also wrote it to suggest a solution that will greatly decrease the popularity of extramarital affairs. By passing laws that make it illegal, we not only send a message that spouses are off-limits as possible lovers, but we also provide betrayed spouses with a legal remedy for appropriate compensation. As it now stands, we do the opposite. Our laws encourage people to have affairs and discourage those who are damaged from defending themselves.

But before we can move forward with new laws, we need to understand how the current laws came to pass. I will address this in the next chapter.

8

The Law Is Wrong
Laws That Encourage Infidelity

I'm fascinated by the way people think. So whenever I talk to legislators about family law, I'm not only interested in the laws they would support or oppose but also in how they come to their conclusions about those laws.

In a meeting I had with one of our leading Minnesota state senators, my objective was to understand his thinking about infidelity and family law. The senator admitted to me that affairs were a scourge on Minnesota families and that children were the primary victims. But he could not support legislation that would make infidelity illegal.

As he struggled to understand his own thinking on that issue, the senator explained it as a conflict between two values. One of his values was to provide children a safe and secure home environment with loving parents. Another value was the right of those parents to make bad choices. He concluded that the right of parents to make bad choices was more important.

"When I married," the senator said, "I did not deprive my wife of the right to choose another romantic relationship, even though it would destroy our family. And to this day, she has that right."

I wanted to be certain that I heard him correctly, and so I asked him to repeat that astonishing statement. After he said it one more time, and I wrote it in my notes, I wondered if his wife felt the same way. Did she understand at the time of their marriage that she was not making a commitment of fidelity to him—or him to her?

Technically, if one were to take the senator's comments to their logical conclusion, we would have no laws at all. All laws are enacted to prevent people from making bad choices. The absolute right to make bad choices simply doesn't exist in civilized society. Yet here I was with a prominent legislator who was arguing from his heart that we should all have the right to make one of the worst choices imaginable—the choice of infidelity.

Changing Law

It wasn't too many centuries ago that someone who had consensual sex with your spouse could be put to death. But now, in most states, they get off scot-free. That's because there have been radical changes in our laws, especially over the past seventy years.

In spite of the fact that it is women who are harmed most by infidelity, it was a woman, Roberta West Nicholson, the only female member of the 1935 Indiana legislature, who led the effort to abolish the laws that offered women protection. At that time there were a growing number of women who wanted to shed the stereotype of being sexually passive and modest, and they wanted the freedom to have affairs. Laws that prevented such behavior got in their way of expressing that "freedom." So their advocate, Representative Nicholson, argued that women didn't need or want such protection from infidelity.

What Nicholson failed to acknowledge was that there are two kinds of women involved in infidelity. There's the lover, who wants the freedom to have affairs with another woman's husband, and there's the wife, who is the ultimate victim of that affair. Nicholson was certainly not speaking for the wife when she argued that women need no protection—she was only speaking for the lover. And technically, she wasn't even speaking for the lover if she had really known how affairs affect a lover. The vast majority of women affected by infidelity, both wives and lovers, are hurt by the affair. So if Roberta Nicholson had truly been an advocate for women, she would have tried to *strengthen* the law against infidelity—not abolish it.

Mistakes in law are common. That's why legislatures all over the world are kept very busy each year rewriting laws to try to correct them. When that Indiana legislature abolished the laws against infidelity in 1935, the mistake was considered "almost unprecedented" by many, including Frederick Kane, a Fordham law professor.[1] Kane reported with alarm that the reasons given for the new law were nothing more than a "smoke screen" for deeper political convictions and that they should never have been tolerated. Even the title of the act itself was bogus, according to Kane. Entitled "An Act to promote public morals,"[2] it was actually an effort to undermine morality.

So how did such weak reasoning prevail in abolishing laws against infidelity in Indiana? One of the primary reasons was that these laws were grouped with another law, breach of promise to marry, which penalized those who broke a marital engagement. It's now almost universally assumed that an engagement is a *proposal*, a tentative decision that can be broken before the final decision is made at the altar, so that law really has no usefulness today. It really *was* a relic of the past, and it deserved to be abolished. But the breach of promise to marry law was unfairly grouped with the laws against infidelity and, by association, tended to make those laws look as if they were obsolete as well.

The real reason for abolishing the breach of promise to marry law was that it was outdated, but that wasn't the argument used to force its demise. Instead, people argued that it created a risk for blackmail and extortion. Now there might be cases somewhere that represented those abuses of the law, but there was never any evidence presented that it was, in fact, used to blackmail or extort. The claim was made, but no one backed up that claim with facts.

This lack of evidence was likely overlooked by most legal scholars because they all agreed that the law just didn't make sense given a common understanding of what an engagement really is—a *proposal* of an agreement. Unfortunately, because the argument seemed to pass muster in the case of breach of promise to marry, it was then assumed that the same argument could be applied to its companion laws against alienation of affections and criminal conversation.

Of course, there were no cases of blackmail or extortion cited as evidence for those laws either. But even if there had been a few cases, why abolish laws that are there to address one of the most egregious forms of human suffering? While breach of promise to marry was a trivial cause of action, there was nothing trivial about infidelity.

Aside from the arguments that some women do not want to be protected from infidelity and that there may be occasional misuse of the law, there were no other arguments against abolishing the laws against alienation of affections and criminal conversation. And no one stepped forward to defend the right of men to be protected by the law. With no one claiming enough harm for the laws to exist, there were essentially no defenders.

Then an amazing thing happened. Rather than the Indiana legislature going back to correct the faulty reasoning in their case, one by one, other states abolished similar laws of their own using the same virtually unprecedented arguments used in Indiana. Illinois and New York followed Indiana in 1935. And by 1950, five more states had abolished the laws of alienation of affections and criminal conversation. Then in the 1970s a new wave of legislation and court decisions added thirty more states and the District of Columbia to the list. All assumed that since other states had rejected those laws on the basis of their vulnerability to blackmail and extortion, the evidence must have existed somewhere. But they didn't provide such evidence themselves.

For example, consider this quote from Minnesota's ruling in 1978.

Chapter 515-S.F.No 997, Section 1. [553.01] BREACH OF PROMISE, ALIENATION OF AFFECTIONS, CRIMINAL CONVERSATION AND SEDUCTION; DECLARATION OF POLICY. Actions based upon alleged alienation of affections, criminal conversation, seduction and breach of contract to marry, have been subject to grave abuses, have caused intimidation and harassment to innocent persons, and have resulted in the perpetration of frauds. It is declared as the public policy of the state that the best interest of the people of the state will be served by the abolition of these causes of action.

In this ruling, the claim of blackmail and extortion was modified to "abuses," "intimidation and harassment," and "perpetration of frauds." But the issues were very similar in that they conveyed the notion that these laws created a climate for misuse. Yet, as was the case in its original 1935 hearing in Indiana, there was absolutely no evidence to support the claim that there had ever been such abuses. The statute passed easily on the mere presumption that other states must have had such evidence.

There are now only eight states remaining that allow a betrayed spouse to sue a lover for damages due to alienation of affections and criminal conversation. And I imagine that number will likely continue to decrease until none are left—unless we do something to change the law to protect marriages.

While most states have abolished these laws using something similar to Indiana's argument of blackmail and extortion, there are other arguments that could be made to support their abolition. So if there is any hope to have them reinstated by state legislatures, we need to clearly understand the weakness of these other arguments as well. That is why I will describe each of them to you in the following pages with the hope that you may be able to start a campaign in your state to reinstate laws that protect marriage.

As I describe the positions of commentators, courts, and legislators over the past seventy years regarding the validity of these arguments, I borrow heavily from the analysis of William Corbett in his brilliant article on this subject that I cited in the last chapter.[3] I'm making this section of the book a little more technical than usual. But if you're serious about understanding influences of current laws on marriage and being a force for change in your state, you'll need all the technical information you can get.

Argument 1: The laws against alienation of affections and criminal conversation are particularly susceptible to blackmail and extortion.

Although there was absolutely no evidence provided to support this original argument, would it be relevant if there had been such evidence? Would a few cases of blackmail and extortion be enough to abolish the laws?

Every law in existence could probably be used for blackmail and extortion. But at what point would you conclude that a law has lost its usefulness because of extortion and blackmail?

We have laws to guard against blackmail and extortion and to protect innocent victims of frivolous and malicious lawsuits. If there had been any special problems regarding these laws, why not improve those laws of protection rather than eliminate the laws in question. To completely abandon a law because it may have been misused occasionally makes no sense at all.

It doesn't take long to imagine why legislators in Indiana would be so fearful of blackmail and extortion regarding affairs. An affair in those days may have ruined their careers, and those having affairs may have actually been blackmailed. But such fear would not be nearly as relevant today when affairs no longer seem to ruin too many political careers. The legislators in 1935 certainly weren't thinking about the suffering of betrayed spouses—but they may have been concerned about their own personal freedom to cheat.

By the way, after many hours of studying cases involving these laws, I have yet to find even one instance in which a spouse threatened blackmail or extortion when alienation of affections or criminal conversation was discovered. I have used the existence of these laws myself (prior to 1978) to encourage clients to threaten a lawsuit if a lover does not end an affair with a married client. But that's not blackmail or extortion—it's reminding the lover of the law.

Argument 2: The laws should be abolished because they treat women as the property of their husbands.

In 1994 the Idaho Supreme Court used this argument to abolish their laws of alienation of affections and criminal

127

conversation. They were right in recognizing that, historically speaking, these two laws originated in a day when a wife's body and services were considered a husband's exclusive property. The original law supposed that when someone had an affair with a married woman, her husband had a right to compensation.

That law was expanded in 1853, however, to include the exclusive rights of a wife to her husband's body and services (*Lumley v. Gye*, 1853). With that expansion, the concept of a spouse as property was put to the test. After all, how could a husband own someone who owned him?

What came from the 1853 decision was that each party to a contract obtained a new form of property. It wasn't money, land, livestock, or a wife—it was an exclusive exchange of services.

Hundreds of years ago it may have been argued that a husband had an exclusive right to his wife's sexual services because she was his property. But when the same claim was extended to a woman's exclusive right to her husband's sexual services, the law lost its property-like features. Instead of a husband owning a wife in marriage, they both agree to provide sexual services to each other—exclusively. That's why the agreement to "forsake all others" is made by both husband and wife in most wedding services.

The marriage agreement describes the service benefits to both parties. As such, it's not much different than most other service agreements. Our laws are very careful to enforce these agreements because the value exchanged is considered a very important form of property. It's not that the wife's body belongs to the husband or the husband's body belongs to the wife. Instead, the "property" in the case of a marriage is the exclusive sexual services each spouse agrees to provide for the other. And as any corporate attorney knows, exclusivity makes a service much more valuable. It could easily be argued that to lose exclusivity is to lose most of the value of a service agreement.

If you have an employee under a no-compete agreement and another company tries to hire that person, you can sue that company for interference with a service agreement—and win. Exclusive marriage agreements should also be protected in the same way. The other company that hires your worker may argue, as Representative Nicholson did, that the exclusive agreement deprives the worker of opportunity. But just as there is a remedy for that problem in the corporate world, there is also a remedy in marriage.

In business, you may quit your job and then wait for a no-compete period of time to elapse, usually six months, before you may work at a similar job for another employer. In marriage, you may divorce—and then you're free to engage in another romantic relationship. The no-compete time gives your employer a chance to address your grievances so you are not as tempted to work for someone else. And in marriage, the time it takes to divorce also gives a spouse a chance to remedy problems that are driving the other spouse away.

It's true that an exclusive right to service inhibits a person's opportunities. Married women who do not cheat on their husbands miss the opportunity to have sex with others. The same is true for the faithful husband. But there is also value in those restrictions—they help keep the marriage stable and secure. If the marriage agreement is reciprocal—if the wife will be faithful on the condition that the husband will be faithful—then the good of mutual fidelity far outweighs the bad of lost sexual opportunities with others. It's a well-documented fact that a stable marriage is a valuable thing for a married couple, for their children, and for society in general. The value of indiscriminate sex, on the other hand, pales in comparison.

While it's true that the original basis of these two laws dealt with a husband's property rights, the laws evolved to become based on the contract rights of *both* husband and wife. Those who argue that the laws should be abolished because wives are no longer the property of their husbands are misinformed or are ignoring this change in the law.

Incidentally, even if one were to argue that property law should not apply at all to the laws of alienation of affections and criminal conversation, there are many other reasons for those laws to exist. But in my judgment, property law *should* still apply in the case of infidelity since a lover is interfering with the fulfillment of a contract.

Argument 3: The laws do not deter infidelity.

The Idaho Supreme Court (1994) used this argument along with the one we just covered. They suggested that when people have affairs, they merely drift into them without considering the legal implications. But they had absolutely no evidence to support their conclusion. No surveys were conducted, and no studies were provided tod defend this most astonishing argument.

While this view may have been inspired by the experience of some of the jurists on the Supreme Court, my experience, as someone who had actually used these laws to prevent affairs from developing, was quite the opposite. In fact, I know that these laws *do* deter infidelity. I've witnessed literally scores of cases having that very outcome. The reason these laws worked so effectively to prevent affairs was because if a third party tried to interfere with a marriage agreement, that party could be sued. In the same way that most companies are careful not to hire away employees who are under an exclusive contract in order to avoid being sued, so these laws deterred a third party from risking the legal penalties of an affair with a married person.

These laws also deterred those who enabled an affair between a spouse and lover. Today there are hundreds of companies on the Internet that have the sole purpose of encouraging spouses to have affairs. Men pay these companies to find other men's wives who are willing to get "frisky." Laws protecting marriage would provide the legal basis for ending such seduction.

Certainly, no law will end all occurrences of a crime, but every law helps reduce such crime if it is enforced. So while it may be true that these laws did not *always* deter infidelity, I witnessed many cases in which they did. When properly enforced, these laws can be quite effective.

Argument 4: The law should not attempt to restrict sexual behavior.

Should the law restrict the consensual sexual activity of adults? That question is often asked with the assumption that the bedroom should be off-limits to legislators. Laws against certain sexual practices are often used to illustrate the ridiculousness of trying to restrict the way adults are to engage in sex. After all, who wants to have sex police checking up on you?

But what if someone is harmed, or even killed, by the act of having sex in a particular way? For example, if there's a high risk of transferring AIDS when engaging in anal sex or if certain sadomasochistic forms of sex end in death for participants, should we create laws to protect people from their own bad judgment—especially when they are the only ones to be hurt?

Some people, like the state senator I interviewed, would say "no," that people should be free to make their own

Just Don't Get Caught?

Family counselors and even some pastors have told me that the damage with infidelity comes not with the act itself but with the discovery of the act. As long as a spouse can keep an affair hidden, there's really no harm in it. So when they discover an affair when counseling a couple, they advise the unfaithful spouse to keep it a secret to avoid causing unbearable harm.

But the day of trusting spouses has long passed, and in our age of technology, affairs are more easily discovered than ever. Most of the affairs I hear about have been discovered through methods that were unknown twenty years ago. Telephone logs, credit card statements, email files, Global Positioning Systems, and even hidden audio and video recorders reveal the comings and goings of just about everyone. And there are a growing number of private investigators available today who will follow your spouse around for a week just to report on whom he or she meets secretly. So the chance of getting away with an affair today is much less likely than it has ever been.

But even if a spouse could get away with it, could the betrayed spouse still be hurt? Many argue that an affair is a great solution for a marriage that has lost its zip. In fact, some have suggested that an affair can actually save a marriage if a spouse needs an extra dose of romance. I debated that issue

poor choices. Yet there are many laws that are designed to protect people from their own destructive behavior. For example, in most states it is illegal to take certain drugs without a doctor's prescription. Even when there is no evidence that such indulgences affect anyone else, you can be imprisoned for the use of those drugs. Seat-belt and helmet laws are also examples of laws that protect people from themselves.

Granted, there are some problems with laws that restrict behavior where only the one responsible for the behavior is hurt. But we still recognize the value of some laws in that area. And if a certain behavior hurts others with two women on the *Sally Jesse Raphael Show* back in 1988. One of them had written a book on the advantages of having an affair, and the other was the publisher of a woman's magazine that supported such behavior.

My position on the subject was that an affair is like heroin, and those having an affair behave very much like heroin addicts. In fact, there is evidence that the physiology of being in an affair is often similar to the physiology of being addicted to heroin. They both provide an emotional experience that is so irresistible that a person loses perspective on what's important in life. I've counseled hundreds of men and women who have given up everything they valued while having an affair—their religious beliefs, their family, their career. It's what I've called "the fog," where nothing seems to be more important than the affair.

Instead of an affair making someone a better spouse, it turns that person into a fool. The betrayed spouse knows that something is terribly wrong, but probing questions are met with denial. That's usually when our new technology offers assistance in discovering the real reason for the sudden drop in everything that's important in marriage—affection, intimate conversation, sex, and companionship.

When that *Sally Jesse Raphael Show* came to a close, I received a standing ovation from the audience of women. Apparently there were enough of them who had suffered through an affair to appreciate my perspective. Even Sally approved.

even indirectly, laws restricting it are much easier to defend. If a behavior hurts others directly, a law against it should be a no-brainer. And that's precisely the case with infidelity. Infidelity is not a harmless sexual act between two consenting adults. Instead, it hurts others in a most devastating way.

Sexual behavior in marriage has a profound effect. When it's exclusive and mutually satisfying, it is the cement that helps bond a couple together for life. But when someone interferes with the marriage agreement and causes a spouse to break his or her vow of faithfulness, the damage is almost beyond reckoning—to the marriage, to the betrayed spouse, to the children, and to society itself. How could anyone view such a devastating loss as a private matter, beyond the jurisdiction of the courts?

Argument 5: Damages due to infidelity are intangible and speculative.

How can the emotional trauma inflicted by infidelity be remedied with money? Even if you agree that infidelity inflicts serious damage, how do you put a price tag on that damage? That's certainly a fair question. But it's not a reason to do away with the laws. Consider all the laws we have today that *do* provide a means for awarding damages for emotional distress that are intentional or due to negligence. It seems that in many cases today, difficult as it might be, we *are* willing to put a price tag on emotional damage.

Admittedly, there are many problems in trying to determine the cost of an emotional injury or even if the emotional injury actually took place. But the courts have consistently viewed these problems as insufficient to refuse the right of recovery for emotional injuries.

> ## Where's the Precedent?
>
> Those who believe that the emotions of love and affection are not subject to monetary damages are simply ignorant of today's judicial practices. It's actually quite common, for example, for courts to award damages for loss of love and affection when an automobile injury prevents one spouse from meeting the intimate needs of the other. So why should an affair be any different?

Those who tried to abolish the laws against infidelity sarcastically called them "heart balm" laws because they were seen as laws that provided monetary damages to make the heart feel better. But that characterization trivialized the incredible suffering that infidelity causes, particularly to women. Besides, the losses suffered by infidelity are not just emotional—they also create significant monetary losses as well as lifestyle upheaval that create additional emotional damage. Given that fact, it's reasonable to have laws that allow for damages to be paid to the affected spouse.

Argument 6: The marriage is worth very little if it's susceptible to an affair. The spouses are to blame, not the third party.

Those who make this argument have had very little experience with spouses who have been unfaithful. Many of the infidelity cases I've witnessed involve people who have had reasonably good marriages prior to their affair but still find themselves emotionally attached to someone else. The affair comes as a complete surprise to them, and they usually don't know what to make of it.

I've spent most of my career trying to help couples understand the importance of creating extraordinary precautions that protect them from an extramarital romantic relationship. Those who travel or work with someone of the opposite sex are most susceptible because they don't understand the risk until it's too late. With the advent of the Internet, there are literally hundreds of thousands of spouses who have wandered into affairs exclusively through the portal of email. These people had no idea that they could fall in love with someone by just sharing their most private thoughts.

Granted, there are people who are looking for an affair because their marriage is romantically unfulfilling, and there are those who are more vulnerable to an affair because of their marital problems. But I've found that many of the marriages infected by infidelity were satisfactory prior to the affair. Sometimes, in an effort to justify bad behavior, an unfaithful spouse will claim to have problems that careful investigation later finds to be pure fiction. Or the problems claimed are trivial, not even coming close to justification of an affair.

But It Takes Two to Tango

But wait . . . isn't the unfaithful spouse as much to blame for an affair as the lover? In many cases, it could be the lover who was the one seduced. Corbett calls this the "superseding cause" argument. When it's difficult to assess blame to one party, it's argued that the law should not address the issue. However, modern law does support partial cause verdicts. And in many cases, the one paying the most damages may turn out to have had only a small role to play in creating the loss. It's a matter of who is in a position to pay for the loss. Since the unfaithful spouse shares financial assets with the betrayed spouse, a financial judgment against that person cannot benefit the betrayed spouse. But a judgment against the lover is a different story.

In a case in which a lover is completely fooled into thinking that a betrayed spouse is unmarried, that person is held faultless by the laws of alienation of affections and criminal conversation. But once the marital status is revealed, if the lover persists in the relationship, he or she is intentionally causing harm to the betrayed spouse.

If the affair is between two married people how could the two betrayed spouses expect to collect damages? Wouldn't it be a lose-lose situation in which each of them would be paying damages to the other? As I mentioned earlier, the lawsuits with which I was personally acquainted never did go to court. The law's value was in stopping the affair. But if the affair somehow persisted in spite of the threatened lawsuit, and both spouses divorced, the law would permit each betrayed spouse to collect damages from the assets of each other's unfaithful spouses. After the divorce, the portion of the marital estate assigned to each unfaithful spouse would be subject to claims.

Regardless of the health of a marriage, however, spouses should be protected from someone who would interfere with their commitment to each other. It's common for a great marriage to suddenly become troubled and then later return to greatness. If marriage predators are lurking about, just waiting for a marriage to weaken long enough to snatch away a spouse and ruin the relationship, shouldn't even the weakest marriages be protected?

Marriage is filled with special responsibilities that require hard work. Raising children properly and earning enough to support them are among some of the most taxing of these responsibilities, and sometimes a spouse simply wants to escape it all. If someone comes along who offers an escape, however shortsighted and foolish it may be, and the temporary escape ruins a marriage and causes untold harm, shouldn't that person be held accountable for the fallout?

Argument 7: Revenge is the real motive for civil action against infidelity, and that's an improper motive.

Another argument made by the Idaho Supreme Court in 1994 to abolish laws against infidelity was that "revenge, which may be a motive for bringing the cause of action, has no place in determining the legal rights between two parties." This seems a reasonable argument on the surface. But should we really abolish all laws that may inspire some to use them for purposes of revenge? For example, if a drunk driver leaves me crippled for life and I want to seek revenge by extracting a painful penalty, should my motive invalidate my case?

We have a judicial system to help prevent people from taking the law into their own hands. Those who have grievances against someone are to present their claims of loss to a judge and then let the law determine the penalty that's fair. But if a type of loss is taken away from the authority of the judicial system, it leaves people who suffer that loss with the sole option of meting out their own form of revenge—something that isn't good for them or for the system as a whole. If revenge really is the primary motive for civil action in the case of infidelity, it would

seem especially important for the judicial system to acknowledge these losses and provide a regulated system
of addressing damage inflicted.

That said, my experience with clients who used the
laws of alienation of affections and criminal conversation
to protect their marriage was that their motivation was
rarely vengeance. It was about shaking the lover loose. In
fact, as I've said repeatedly, I never did see a case actually
make it to court. When it became apparent that a civil
lawsuit could be filed for damages, the affair was ended.
If revenge had been the motive in any of those cases, the
betrayed spouse would have gone ahead with a trial even
though the lover had ended the relationship.

Argument 8: Laws against marital interference can punish free speech.

When it comes to interference of any contract, is verbal
persuasion allowed under the first amendment of the right
to free speech? For example, if you had a no-compete
agreement with a company and, as your counselor, I advise
you to break that agreement and find another job with
a competing company, could I be held liable? According
to the law, yes.

The first amendment does not allow us to say anything
we want to say under the protection of free speech. If
what we say encourages someone to break the law, we
can be prosecuted for conspiracy to commit that crime
and suffer the same penalty as the lawbreaker. Because
the marital agreement provides for sexual exclusivity,
advice to break that agreement falls outside the bounds
of protected free speech.

While we don't find too many qualified counselors recommending affairs to their clients, we do see an increasing
number of books and Internet websites that encourage
infidelity among spouses. From my perspective, if it can

be proven that a crime was committed due to the influence of a particular website, those responsible for it should be prosecuted. This should be true whether the crime was murder, rape, or marital infidelity.

Professional rules are already in place forbidding most counselors from encouraging their clients to have affairs with them. That's because it's common knowledge that counselors hold a position of authority over their clients, and clients are relatively easy to seduce in a patient-client relationship. It's also known that such affairs can be very destructive to the client. A psychologist in Minnesota will lose his or her license to practice if this rule is violated, even if the client willingly engages in such an affair.

But it isn't just affairs with counselors that are destructive. *Any* affair always harms the betrayed spouse, and it usually harms the unfaithful spouse as well. So even if a counselor were to advise an affair with someone else, most professionals would regard the advice as being very irresponsible because affairs do not solve personal problems—they create problems.

Argument 9: There is no state money available for additional civil cases.

As I mentioned earlier, when I used the threat of alienation of affections and criminal conversation to shake loose a lover, not a single case actually reached the court. The laws themselves helped me prevent affairs from developing and helped stop those already taking place. That's what laws usually do—they help prevent harmful behavior.

But I'm sure there will be a few cases that reach the courts if these laws are reinstated. We can estimate how many of these cases there will be by looking at those that came to the court's attention prior to abolishment. A survey of all such civil lawsuits in Minnesota prior to

139

1978 gives us an estimate of how much burden they were to the courts. As it turns out, the percentage of all civil cases that addressed adultery was very small. While every law adds some cost to the court system, these laws were a very minor part of the whole when they were enforced.

Still, I will admit that there could be a disproportionately large number of new lawsuits filed if the laws are reenacted. That's because the rate of infidelity has soared since the laws were abolished. With no laws forbidding such behavior, an ever-increasing number of marriages suffer from affairs. For a few years, therefore, we may very well see an unusually large number of cases reach the courts because the problem has grown out of control.

It's my opinion, however, that once the laws are again in place and the public is aware of legal consequences of affairs, there will be a return to a relatively small number of cases that are actually prosecuted. Along with that reduction of cases, we would also see a great reduction in affairs and the tremendous harm they create.

The Bottom Line

Ultimately it comes down to the questions: Is the problem of infidelity important enough for our laws to address? Are the damages caused by an affair significant enough to claim?

The irony of our present situation is that those who led the charge to abolish laws against infidelity were mostly women. Yet my experience counseling both men and women who are victims of affairs clearly points to women and their children as suffering the greater emotional trauma. And when affairs lead to divorce, women also tend to be the most seriously injured, being left with overwhelming responsibility and very little financial support.

It's not that men are unaffected by their wife's affair. Quite the contrary; they also usually report it as one of the worst experiences of their lives. But those I've counseled usually bounce back emotionally much quicker than women, especially after the affair is over and their marriages are recovering.

Why would anyone want to eliminate laws that protect so many women and children from such emotionally devastating behavior? What reasons could possibly justify abolishing a shield of protection to these vulnerable people? It simply doesn't make sense. And it leaves us with our work cut out for us if we are to protect marriages from infidelity in today's culture.

9

How to Affair-Proof Your Marriage

Overcoming Cultural
and Legal Obstacles
to Romantic Exclusivity

An affair is devastating to a betrayed spouse. It's one of the most painful experiences that he or she could ever endure. In fact, most betrayed spouses can't think of a single tragedy that is worse for them than the affair.

Consider these examples (the names have been changed to protect their identity):

Nancy's father was murdered, and her mother died of a very aggressive cancer in the same year. Both were very close to Nancy, and their sudden deaths were devastating to her. But she reported that the pain she suffered from her husband's affair was far more devastating.

Cindy had been sexually molested by her father in her early teens. Yet her husband's one-year affair with a woman he met while away on business created far more trauma for her than her father's irresponsible behavior.

Julie was raped by a stranger when she attended college. She told us that the rape paled in comparison to her struggle with her husband's two-year affair with a female co-worker.

Robin was gang-raped when she was twenty-three. She reported that her husband's one-year affair with a woman he met at the local bar was much more difficult to overcome than the physical and emotional damage from the rape.

Chad's six-year-old son died in a backyard accident. He said that the pain he suffered from his wife's affair with a neighbor was far greater than the pain from his son's tragic death.

Sylvia's younger sister was raped and murdered by a stranger when Sylvia was twenty-one. But her husband's five-month affair with a co-worker caused her to suffer more than the brutal death of her younger sister, whom she cared for very deeply.

These are just a few of the testimonials that we have recorded when counseling the victims of infidelity at the Marriage Builders Counseling Center. Scores of others have told me the same thing. A spouse's affair is just about the worst experience in anyone's life. But it's not just betrayed spouses who are injured by infidelity. It's also very painful for their children. Friends and members of the extended family are usually hurt as well. And the unfaithful spouse and the lover are also hurt by the experience. It almost always causes them to suffer acute depression, often with thoughts of suicide.

So with all the sadness that infidelity creates, why do so many people do it? And why would our laws and culture encourage it?

I strongly believe that the primary reason there are so many affairs is that our brains are wired to have them. Our instinct to procreate is probably at the root of it all. But whatever the cause, most of us would have an affair if we were given an opportunity to do so, in spite of the suffering it causes.

And that may have something to do with why our laws and culture encourage infidelity. It's such a common problem, that legislators may have come to view it as a necessary evil. In fact, since they're even *more* likely to have affairs than most because in their positions of power, why would they want to pass legislation that would punish their own predispositions?

So even though I encourage you to help change our laws and culture to protect families from infidelity, for the foreseeable future you will have to create a protective shield around your family without those changes. As I mentioned earlier, my own research has provided me with evidence that about 60 percent of all marriages experience this tragedy. But what about the remaining 40 percent? How do they escape? And what can you do to escape the tragedy of infidelity?

I'm convinced that most of these couples do what my wife, Joyce, and I have done—they've inoculated their marriage from infidelity. They don't simply use willpower to avoid affairs. They take precautions that are necessary to guard their marriage. Join Joyce and me and the 40 percent who inoculate their marriage from this threat. Doesn't it make sense to take whatever precautions are necessary to avoid what may turn out to be your life's worst experience?

Expanding Circles

In the age of the Internet, friends become a very broad category for many of us because friends are no longer limited to your neighbors or those in close physical proximity to you. Total strangers living thousands of miles away can become friends within an hour. And these new friends can meet your need for intimate conversation and recreational companionship through chat rooms, email, and Internet games. Do you and your spouse talk as much and as deeply as you talk to people on the Internet? If not, watch out. As you probably know, an affair through the Internet is becoming one of the most dangerous risks of owning a computer.

Where Does It Start?

In order to affair-proof your marriage, you need to first understand how affairs usually begin. Friends and co-workers are the most likely people to tempt you to have an affair. That's because they are usually the ones who are in the best position to meet your most intimate emotional needs.

While it's true that some affairs take place even when a marriage is rock solid, they're more likely to occur when a couple is disillusioned with marriage. More specifically, a couple is more vulnerable to affairs when the romantic relationship that motivated them to marry comes to an end and they stop meeting each other's intimate emotional needs.

Since there are so many who don't know how to restore their romantic relationship or, like Michael Gurian (see chapter 6), don't believe that it's possible to restore romance in marriage, they are left with affairs as their only hope for romance. Women who have affairs usually need more affection and intimate conversation from their husbands, while men usually need more sexual fulfillment and recreational companionship from their wives. When someone meets those needs outside of marriage, that person becomes irresistible because those needs are so strong.

I wrote *His Needs, Her Needs: Building an Affair-Proof Marriage*[1] to warn couples of this danger and help them inoculate their marriage from infidelity by encouraging them to meet each other's intimate emotional needs. My message is simple: If you don't meet all of each other's four intimate emotional needs, someone else is likely to meet those you miss. When that happens, your entire world will come crashing down on top of you.

But meeting each other's intimate emotional needs is only half of what it takes to inoculate your marriage from an affair. While marital dissatisfaction is a factor in most affairs, it's not the whole story. Sometimes an affair can take place even when a couple meets each other's needs and are deeply in love. These affairs are particularly troubling to couples because they don't know what they could have done to make their marriage any more solid than it was. But the Love Bank explains how it can happen—and how to protect your marriage from these surprise attacks.

Spouses rarely intend to be unfaithful. In fact, most adulterous relationships begin as an innocent friendship. When a spouse and a friend talk to each other and share recreational time together, they don't do it to meet intimate emotional needs and build Love Bank balances—it just turns out that way. But whether or not it's intended, if enough deposits are made, when the romantic love threshold is breached, an intense feeling of romantic love is triggered, even when you are already in love with your spouse.

To avoid this early stage of an affair and the risk of falling in love with someone outside of marriage, I advise you to take these crucial precautions:

1. Limit your most intimate conversation to your spouse. Make your spouse your favorite person with whom to share your deepest thoughts and feelings and prevent those of the opposite sex (outside of

your family) from knowing about any dissatisfaction you may be having in your marriage.

2. Limit your most enjoyable leisure or recreational activities to those you share with your spouse. Make your spouse your favorite recreational companion and avoid recreational activities with those of the opposite sex (outside of your family). (See chapter 3 for a description of intimate conversation and recreational companionship.)

Intimate conversation and recreational companionship often slip under the radar when spouses consider their risk for an affair. They are often seen as benign, especially when compared to the other two intimate emotional needs—affection and sexual fulfillment. It goes without saying that spouses should not be intimately affectionate outside of marriage, giving intimate gifts, cuddling, or kissing someone passionately. And sexual acts are most certainly viewed as a violation of marital commitment. But spouses often fail to see the danger in intimate conversation and recreational companionship until it's too late.

At first glance, most couples see my precautions as overly cautious and overly restrictive. After all, some say, just because you're married, must you be kept isolated from the rest of humanity? But I'm not suggesting isolation; I'm suggesting that unless the four needs of intimacy are met exclusively in marriage, an affair is likely to develop.

It's just too risky to avoid these precautions, especially when you consider how much suffering it causes those you promised to care for and protect. When you let someone else meet any of your intimate emotional needs, you'll tend to fall in love with that person. And then if you express your attraction to that person, you'll be in even deeper trouble. A seed will have been planted that quickly grows out of control.

Ending It Before It Starts

If you have not followed the precautions I've suggested and a relationship gets to a point where you and another person have feelings of attraction toward each other, I have two more guidelines that will help you nip your romance in the bud.

1. Never tell someone of the opposite sex other than your spouse that you find him or her attractive. Instead, if you find someone particularly attractive, tell your spouse how you feel about that person.
2. If someone of the opposite sex ever tells you that he or she finds you attractive, say nothing about how you feel toward that person. But let your spouse know what that person said to you.

When you know that someone of the opposite sex is attracted to you, or you are attracted to that person, you are at a crossroad: either take the next step in developing that relationship, or tell your spouse about it, end the relationship, and rebuild your marriage.

Honesty helps a couple end a potential affair before it goes too far. I always advise spouses who find themselves falling in love with someone to tell their spouse everything. From that day forward, they should avoid contact with the other person, and the couple should spend much more time meeting each other's intimate emotional needs.

Of course the other spouse should cooperate in rebuilding their romantic relationship. If the revelation of a threatened affair makes the other spouse less willing to rebuild a romantic relationship, it tends to encourage the affair rather than nip it in the bud. But at the very least, honesty gives the other spouse a clear choice at a time when an affair has not yet taken place: Do we restore our romantic relationship, or do we risk the disaster of an affair?

Some counselors advise spouses not to share with each other their feelings of attraction to someone else. How very foolish. Don't they realize how many affairs could be avoided if spouses were to share their deepest feelings with each other—especially their feelings toward those of the opposite sex?

Past the Point of Prevention

Unfortunately, most tempted spouses don't follow the path that leads away from an affair. Instead, they tell the prospective lover that they're not simply attracted but that they're falling in love—precisely the opposite of what I recommend. They write love letters to each other that express both their love and their guilt: "I find myself thinking about you often and wish I could be with you. I feel so guilty and ashamed of these feelings, but nevertheless, they are there. I try not to think about you, but I do."

Once this revelation of being in love is expressed by either person, an affair is usually off and running. Even if one of them has never given their relationship a single romantic thought, he or she begins to see the other person in an entirely new way. As their Love Bank accounts grow, the affair usually graduates from intimate conversation and recreational companionship to affection and sexual fulfillment, making their accounts grow even faster. The couple usually knows that what they're doing is wrong, yet they feel compelled to draw ever closer to each other.

Although we usually consider sex as the primary motive for an affair, it's actually not the driving force—intimate conversation and recreational companionship are usually the real culprits. In fact, most people who have affairs regard sex as a minor player. What they appreciate most about the relationship is how they have bonded through their conversation and leisure activities with each other. Still, sex and affection are usually the inevitable outcome, and since they work best with great conversation, the sex and affection are also great. And once they are added to the mix, so many love units get deposited that the couple cannot imagine losing each other. They both become addicted to the relationship.

There is no emotion more powerful than romantic love. People have abandoned their careers, their children, their religion, their security, and their health because of it. Try talking to a man who is in love with his secretary about the suffering he is causing his wife and children. Try explaining to him how he will lose his job, his money, and his self-respect. You find yourself talking to a man with half a brain—a man who seems possessed. What's going on that causes him to lose all of his perspective on life? It's nothing more than the feeling of love. But that feeling is one of the most compelling feelings we have, and we will do almost anything to get it and keep it.

Once an affair is up and running, it magnifies unfaithful spouses' dissatisfaction with their marriage. They talk about how incompatible they are with their spouse and how compatible they are with their lover. Their addiction makes marital reconciliation seem impossible. Many have told me that they'd rather commit suicide together with their lover than return to their spouse. Some try to justify their affair by claiming that their feelings of love are a signal from God to abandon their marriage and rush into this new relationship. But it's no signal from God. Instead, it's the way our emotions mindlessly encourage us to spend more time with those who meet our intimate emotional needs. And it's that need to be together as often as possible that usually exposes the affair.

Telltale Signs

Betrayed spouses usually sense a problem when an affair begins. When they are with their unfaithful spouse, an emotional distance usually prevails. All four intimate emotional needs are more difficult to give and receive. In many cases, intimacy in marriage becomes so bad that unfaithful spouses request a separation to "sort things out." They usually say that they're confused as to how they feel or have lost their feeling of love toward their spouse.

But the clearest evidence of an affair is the unfaithful spouse's excuses for time away from home—having to work late, impulsive trips to the store, and unexplained absences from work—they all become increasingly difficult to believe. Telephone records and credit card receipts are carefully hidden, for if they're found, they often reveal the affair.

Of course if a spouse has a career that requires frequent travel, the time it takes to maintain an affair is much easier to conceal. That's why affairs are more highly associated with careers in airline travel, long-distance trucking, sales, marketing, and corporate consulting. Any career that keeps spouses from being together at night not only increases the risk for an affair but also makes affairs more difficult to detect.

While a betrayed spouse often suspects the affair, the unfaithful spouse usually denies it vigorously. It usually takes solid evidence to get an unfaithful spouse to admit the truth, and even then, a confession may not be forthcoming. One betrayed spouse I counseled caught her husband in their bed having sex with a neighbor. After the neighbor grabbed her clothes and ran from the house, the wife asked her husband for an explanation. Instead of admitting his mistake, he told his wife that she was delusional—what she thought she'd seen had never really happened.

By the time people get themselves into this mess, it becomes very difficult to end it. My experience is that only about 15 percent of those who find themselves mired in an affair can end it the right way—by saying good-bye to the lover and never seeing or talking to that person again. The other 85 percent cannot take that intelligent and thoughtful step. Instead, they continue the affair until it dies a natural death. And that's the way almost all affairs end—they die. That's because they usually don't make sense, and when they're exposed to the light of day, they unravel. They're usually held together by pure fantasy and very little logic. So when emotional attraction begins to falter, at least one party realizes that the affair was a serious mistake.

I firmly believe that all of us would have an affair under certain conditions and none of us would have one under other conditions. In other words, none of us can be trusted unless certain precautions are taken. But when the precautions are in place, all of us can be trusted. So the precautions I recommend help create the conditions that make an affair essentially impossible—they help couples avoid the temptation of an affair. And with all the suffering that an affair can create for a family, don't those precautions that I mentioned earlier make more sense to you now?

Restoration Is Possible

If you follow the precautions I recommend, you'll never experience the tragedy of an affair. But what if you have not followed them? What if you or your spouse is mired in an affair? Can your marriage be saved?

I've spent most of my professional life helping couples restore their marriage after an affair. It can be done if a couple follows a very narrow path to recovery. I've written a book with my daughter, Jennifer Harley Chalmers, describing that path—*Surviving an Affair*.[2] In the book we recommend three steps you must take if you hope to restore your marriage following an affair.

Step 1: Never see or communicate with a former lover.

Once an affair is first revealed, whether it's discovered or admitted, the betrayed spouse is usually in a state of shock. Panic is often the first reaction, but it's quickly followed by anger. Divorce and sometimes even murder and suicide are contemplated. But after some time passes (usually about three weeks), most couples decide that they will try to pull together and save their marriage.

The one having an affair is in no position to bargain, but he or she usually tries anyway. The bargaining effort usually boils down to somehow keeping the lover in the loop. You would think that the unfaithful spouse would be so aware of his or her weaknesses, and so aware of the pain inflicted, that every effort would be made to avoid further contact with the lover as an act of thoughtfulness to the stunned spouse. But instead, the unfaithful spouse often argues that the relationship was "only sexual" or was "emotional but not sexual," or some other outrageous claim that is supposed to make continued contact with the lover okay.

Most betrayed spouses intuitively understand that all contact with a lover must end for life. Permanent separation not only helps prevent a renewal of the affair, but it is also a crucial gesture of consideration to someone who has been through hell because of it. What betrayed spouse would ever want his or her unfaithful spouse to

How to End It

How should an unfaithful spouse tell his or her lover that their relationship is over? If left to his or her own devices, many would take a Caribbean cruise to say those final good-byes. So I usually intervene to prevent him or her from making matters worse. I recommend that the final good-bye be in the form of a letter—not in person or even by telephone.

My advice is to write a final letter in a way that ends the affair decisively and encourages the betrayed spouse. It should begin with a statement of how selfish it was to cause those he or she loves so much pain, and while marital reconciliation cannot completely repay the offense, it is the right thing to do. A statement should be made about how much the unfaithful spouse cares about his or her spouse and family and, for their protection, has decided to completely end the relationship with the lover. He or she has promised never to see or communicate with the lover again in life and asks the lover to respect that promise. Nothing should be said about how much the lover will be missed. After the letter is written, the betrayed spouse should read and approve it before it is sent.

see or communicate with a former lover at work or in some other activity?

In spite of career sacrifices, friendships, and issues relating to children's schooling, I am adamant in recommending that there be no contact with a former lover for life. That may even mean a move to another state. But to do otherwise fails to recognize the nature of addiction and its cure.

Once the lover is permanently removed from the unfaithful spouse's life, the couple is faced with another problem: withdrawal. This is the emotional reaction to the loss of something that has provided incredible pleasure. It's what an alcoholic feels when he or she makes a commitment never to drink again. It's also similar to the grief that comes from the loss of a loved one. Not only does the unfaithful spouse miss what it was the lover did for him or her, meeting intimate emotional needs, but the unfaithful spouse also misses the person he or she had come to love.

Since the symptoms of withdrawal often are very intense, I usually suggest that antidepressant medication be used to help alleviate these symptoms. While the most intense symptoms of withdrawal usually last only about three weeks, in some cases they can linger for six months or longer before they start to fade.

While going through withdrawal, it is likely that the commitment to remain separated from a lover will be broken unless extreme measures are taken to avoid it. That's because the emotional reaction of withdrawal is so painful. So a plan should be in place to guarantee that there be no contact. Getting rid of a home computer and cell phone, quitting a job, and even moving to another state are but a few of the extraordinary precautions that I've found necessary to prevent a relapse. Since many of those who have had an affair do not want to divorce, they are willing to do whatever is necessary to break their addiction to their lover. And as most counselors of addicts know, absolute separation from the source of the addiction is crucial. If a contact is made, it throws the unfaithful spouse back to the beginning of withdrawal, and the time it takes to overcome the feelings of grief begin all over again.

Step 2: Create a plan to restore your marital relationship.

If a marriage was disappointing before an affair, imagine how disappointing it would be after an affair. The marital problems that helped create the affair are not only still present, but now there's the affair itself that makes matters much worse. So the plan to restore a marital relationship must be very carefully constructed. And one of the most important parts of that plan is how to deal with the emotional reactions left over from the affair.

Should the plan to restore marriage begin with an apology and forgiveness? There are many who advocate both. They say that reconciliation cannot begin unless the unfaithful spouse expresses sincere regret and the betrayed spouse forgives (some have even suggested forgiveness even without an apology).

My experience in helping couples recover after an affair, however, has taught me that neither is necessary in the beginning. What's necessary for recovery is the implementation of a plan that guarantees that both spouses give each other the extraordinary care I described in chapters 3 through 5. Then, when that care is provided, sincere regret and sincere forgiveness usually follow. In other words, the time to forgive and trust an unfaithful spouse is not the moment he or she decides to give the marriage a chance to succeed. It's when that spouse has proven to be trustworthy that forgiveness is most appropriate.

Besides, in the beginning of recovery it's very common for unfaithful spouses to feel unremorseful. They don't think they should get all the blame—they believe the betrayed spouse should share some of it for failing to provide the extraordinary care that was promised. It's also common for the betrayed spouse to feel that forgiveness is premature. So what good is an apology if it's insincere, and what good is forgiveness that is deemed inappropriate?

Another mistake couples are tempted to make is to dwell on the affair. I strongly suggest that once the details of the affair have been exposed (who the lover was, how the affair developed, what was done during the affair, and how it ended), it should not be mentioned again. One of the enemies of intimate conversation is to dwell on mistakes of the past. Since an affair is one of the biggest mistakes you'll ever make in life, any reference to it during your conversations are sure to be unpleasant for both of you.

As I've already mentioned, your plan for recovery should be to give each other the extraordinary care you promised on your wedding day: meet each other's intimate emotional needs, overcome Love Busters, and create a mutually enjoyable lifestyle with the Policy of Joint Agreement.

Since your emotional reactions will tend to sabotage your efforts, your plan may need some outside help to hold you accountable to complete the program of recovery. The betrayed spouse is often tempted to throw in the towel at any sign of reluctance on the part of the unfaithful spouse. And the unfaithful spouse is equally skittish. So your plan should address motivational problems you are likely to encounter.

Your plan should also allow for sufficient time to get the job done. My advice is to schedule as much time with each other as possible each week so that you'll be able to learn how to provide extraordinary care. But I've found that there is a minimum amount of time that's necessary—fifteen hours a week. If you schedule less time, you won't succeed. And if you skip a week, you'll lose ground.

Step 3: Complete your plan to restore your marital relationship.

Having helped thousands of couples restore their love for each other after an affair, I've found that it usually takes about two years of dedicated effort to get the job done. And the most difficult part is usually the beginning. If a couple can stick to their plan during the first three months of recovery, the next twenty-one months are usually much less effort, and much more enjoyable.

By the end of the two years, the unfaithful spouse has sincerely apologized, the betrayed spouse has forgiven him or her, trust is restored, and they are in love with each other. They are not only providing each other extraordinary care, but they have put in place the extraordinary precautions to avoid an affair in the future.

Of the three basic elements of extraordinary care that couples must learn to give each other, I usually encourage them to begin by learning to meet each other's intimate emotional needs. Next, they should learn to meet the other six important emotional needs. They should also guarantee each other's safety by eliminating Love Busters. And finally, they should create a lifestyle of mutual enjoyment by following the Policy of Joint Agreement whenever they make decisions.

My books *His Needs, Her Needs: Building an Affair-proof Marriage* and *Love Busters: Overcoming Habits that Destroy Romantic Love*, as well as the workbook that goes with those books, *Five Steps to Romantic Love*, were written to help couples learn to provide extraordinary care for each other. There are thousands of couples who have restored their marriage after an affair by using these resources.

In addition, I have developed home-study courses to go with *His Needs, Her Needs* and *Love Busters*. Those courses are available through the Marriage Builders Bookstore (www.marriagebuilders.com).

Suppressing the Destructive Instinct of Infidelity

When I decided to take precautions to avoid an affair in my marriage with Joyce, I was making an effort to suppress my instinct to have an affair. And when I recommend precautions to every married couple, I'm encouraging them to suppress their instincts.

But we live in a culture in which we're led to believe that the suppression of instincts is somehow wrong, particularly when it's applied to avoiding affairs. Sometimes

Tradition Gone Awry

There's something wrong with traditional bachelor parties—the last chance for unlimited sexual expression. What a way to begin a marriage! Instead of celebrating the anticipation of the very fulfilling sexual relationship that he and his bride will share exclusively with each other, a groom chooses to wallow in the slime of perverted sex. Groomsmen make it seem as if he's about to lose everything valuable in life.

But nothing could be farther from the truth. What a man leaves at the bachelor's party has no value to him at all, and what he's about to receive is incredibly valuable to him. When a man and woman agree to a lifelong, exclusive sexual relationship, they are creating the very best of what a sexual relationship has to offer. It not only is sexually fulfilling, but the offspring created by their union are born into an environment of safety and security—parents who love each other and love their children.

those who have just had an affair think that precautions are actually punishment for bad behavior. The truth is, these precautions are not punishment—they're common sense. If every married couple were to fully understand the high risk of an affair and the incredible pain it creates, everyone would be taking these precautions. Who wants to nurture an instinct that causes us to unleash unbearable pain and suffering on those we care for most?

If our marriages are to be successful, sexual expression must be limited to our spouse and suppressed toward all others. But this restraint does not cause any loss of sexual enjoyment. On the contrary, it leads to very passionate and frequent sexual experiences for married couples who provide extraordinary care to each other. How can anyone who cares about themselves and others possibly justify the right to unlimited sexual expression? Who would ever suggest that it's a good idea when the devastating consequences are so apparent? I have already mentioned the overwhelming emotional consequences, but there are also sexually transmitted diseases and unwanted pregnancies to consider. There are a host of problems that sexual promiscuity creates.

For those who choose to avoid sexual promiscuity, sexual exclusivity requires sexual accessibility. If marriage means limiting sex to the husband and wife, they must both be willing to meet each other's sexual needs. They must cooperate with each other so that neither feels frustrated. But there comes a time in many marriages when sex becomes unfulfilling for one spouse. In some marriages, the unfulfilled spouse is simply reluctant to make love, giving excuses to put it off or to make it quick. In other cases, he or she simply refuses to make love. I've spent much of my professional career straightening out these failures that are usually brief but very distressing. After all, sex is one of the most powerful needs that we have.

But an affair is not the answer to a spouse's sexual reluctance. The answer is for a couple to come to grips with their promise to provide extraordinary care for each other. And that means being a sexually skilled and responsive partner. Sexual reluctance usually means that the pleasure of making love is not mutual—only one spouse enjoys the experience. The solution to this problem, along with all other problems regarding the meeting of emotional needs, is to recognize the crucial importance of meeting the need in a way that's enjoyable for both parties. Spouses have a responsibility to meet each other's need for sexual fulfillment, but it must be done in a way that is mutually enjoyable.

Some spouses have come to my office threatening to separate if problems of intimacy are not resolved in their marriage. They refuse to continue living with a spouse who doesn't meet their needs for intimate conversation, recreational companionship, affection, or sexual fulfillment. That's a strategy that actually makes good sense as a last resort—far more sense than to have an affair. A separation can give both spouses a new perspective on their problem so they can address it with wisdom and energy. But an affair does just the opposite. It makes spouses feel that they should give up on each other. While I've seen thousands of couples resolve their sexual problems after an affair, it would have been much easier, and far less traumatic, to have solved the problem without the affair—even if they would have had to separate for a while.

But before taking the drastic step of a separation, which can lead to divorce or infidelity, I advise couples to first try to find a counselor or mentoring couple who is skilled in motivating reluctant spouses to meet intimate emotional needs in marriage. I know how difficult it can be to reach a spouse who has no interest in restoring a romantic relationship, because I try to do that almost every day. But I also know that it can be done in most cases.

It's not just intimate conversation, recreational companionship, affection, or sexual fulfillment that makes affairs appealing. It's also the other elements of extraordinary care that are usually provided. In an affair, lovers try to avoid hurting each other, and they make decisions with each other's interests in mind. When that level of care is missing in marriage but present in an affair, it's very difficult to resist the affair. But if your marriage also provides extraordinary care, you'll see affairs for what they really are—your worst nightmare.

We live in a society that does not value fidelity the way it used to be valued. Our laws encourage affairs, books are written to show you how to get away with an affair, and websites on the Internet will help you find a lover. But you can avoid that tragedy by joining Joyce and me along with millions of other couples who have affair-proofed our marriages. We provide extraordinary care in our marriages, and we prevent anyone of the opposite sex from meeting any of our intimate emotional needs. That's what it takes to maintain a traditional marriage at a time when it's been under unprecedented attack.

PART 3

"TILL DEATH DO US PART"

Permanence

10

When Is It Time to Call It Quits?

Divorce and Its Dire Consequences

One of the promises a bride and groom make at their wedding is the promise to remain married "until death do us part." And that promise makes quite a bit of sense, especially if a couple expects to raise children. Few, if any, spouses would go through with the wedding if they expected to divorce once children entered the picture. After all, what spouse would want to have the burden of raising his or her offspring without the support and help of the other spouse? And what child would want to be raised by parents who are divorced?

Of course, permanence in marriage has benefits that go far beyond those involved in raising offspring. Even a childless couple is better off if their relationship lasts for a lifetime because they will be healthier, wealthier, and happier than their divorced counterparts—even those who remarry after the divorce.

Couples who stay married for life are healthier because they encourage each other to live healthier lives and because they care for each other when they're sick. They are wealthier because they earn more money, especially if they have dual careers. These couples also spend money more efficiently than they would if they were separated because together they get more for the money they earn. And finally, they are happier because they meet many emotional needs that can only be met by someone who cares deeply for another. Affection, intimate conversation, recreational companionship, sexual fulfillment, admiration—each of these can only be met by someone else. And those needs are met best in a *permanent* relationship of extraordinary care.

After forming a partnership in which each spouse specializes in unique skills, a husband and wife create a higher quality of life than either could create by themselves because of their greater efficiency. And the longer a couple remains married, the more skilled they become, providing a host of services for each other, both great and small.

That specialization in marriage leads to interdependence. As they share responsibilities, they need each other to perform various tasks. And the longer a couple is married, the more they need each other. As they grow together, they have an increasing need for the services that each brings to the relationship. It's as though they become one, with two parts functioning to the advantage of the whole. Even their brains grow to accommodate each other.

That's why the death of a spouse is usually so traumatic. When a couple grows together, they cannot easily replace what they do for each other. After one is gone, the quality of life they've built together is suddenly lost. Even

Independence Is *Not* Ideal

Some people are troubled by the fact that a healthy marriage leads to interdependence. They've witnessed how interdependence can lead to overwhelming sadness and desperation when a spouse dies. And in other cases, they've seen how *dependence* of any kind can make them victims of control and abuse.

So they tend to make a fateful decision—they try to be *independent*. Many decide to live together instead of marrying. And those who marry try to be self-sufficient to avoid the risk of becoming dependent on a controlling and abusive spouse. But both of those strategies, cohabiting and trying to be independent in marriage, are actually primary causes of abuse. It has been demonstrated in a host of studies that those who cohabitate, or who try to live independently while married, experience much greater abuse and a higher rate of divorce than those who learn to be interdependent on each other. That's because such couples fail to provide each other with the extraordinary care that's promised in a marriage of interdependency.

If a couple provides the extraordinary care to each other that I've described, there is no risk of control and abuse. And divorce makes absolutely no sense at all. When a husband and wife meet each other's important emotional needs, prevent themselves from hurting each other, and create a lifestyle that they both enjoy, permanence is the logical outcome. There's no reason to divorce.

But when they have failed to provide extraordinary care for each other, there's plenty of reason to divorce. When they fail to meet each other's emotional needs, fail to avoid hurting each other, and fail to take each other into account when making decisions, all they can think about is how to end a very disappointing and painful experience. They married because they expected that extraordinary care from each other, and when it's not forthcoming, they usually divorce.

another partner cannot fill the void very easily—there's too much to learn.

We are wired as human beings to thrive in a *permanent* relationship of extraordinary care. Yet couples give up that decisive advantage when they decide to divorce.

167

Divorce Has Consequences

The sad reality is that far too many couples fail to care for each other. They neglect to meet each other's emotional needs, they deliberately hurt each other, and they make thoughtless lifestyle decisions. They make their relationship so unpleasant that a divorce seems to be the only reasonable escape.

It leaves them with a dilemma. Should they continue to suffer from an unhappy marriage so their children will be more successful, or should they end their suffering with divorce and cast their children's future to the wind?

Although divorce may appear to be the most sensible way to end the problems of marriage, it has consequences that make those problems seem almost trivial in comparison. Divorce makes spouses poorer economically and more desperate emotionally. Those of us who know and work with divorced parents are witness to the fact that their divorce did not solve their problems. These parents, it seems, have sacrificed the happiness and success of their children for nothing. It rarely ends the suffering caused by a bad marriage because divorce creates a host of new problems that are even more painful, especially for children.

Don't get me wrong. I'm not advocating bad marriages. But a bad marriage is usually far less painful to spouses and their children than a divorce. For example, recent studies suggest that children are five times less likely to live in poverty and twelve times less likely to spend time in jail if their parents remain married—even if the marriage is unfulfilling.

There are a host of other advantages as well for children who are raised in the context of a permanent marriage. Such children are healthier, more successful in school, less likely to abuse drugs and alcohol, less likely to suffer from mental illness, and less likely to be sexually or physically abused. They are also more likely to have a successful marriage of their own.

Children aren't the only ones who benefit from parents who stay together. Permanent marriage offers plenty of advantages to adults as well. They will also be happier, healthier, and wealthier if they simply avoid divorce. And they can be happily married if they follow my recommendations of giving each other the extraordinary care they promised and expected from each other.

That's really all it takes to be happily married throughout life—extraordinary care. If all couples were to provide that level of care for each other, we wouldn't even be discussing divorce.

So should an unhappy couple stay married? Absolutely. But why have an unhappy marriage? As long as you'll be together anyway, why not turn it into a happy marriage? And if you're staying together for the sake of the children, why not show them how to be thoughtful adults by being thoughtful to each other?

When the rate of divorce skyrocketed in the 1960s and '70s, I knew that dire consequences were on the horizon. But very few scientific studies had been conducted to investigate the effects of divorce on families. At the time, without any evidence, most of my colleagues felt that the high rate of divorce was a sign of social progress and that research would find divorce to be beneficial. Now, forty years later, it is clear that the opposite is true. More than ten thousand studies have shown that divorce seriously diminishes the happiness and opportunity of both parents and children, even when compared with an unhappy marriage.

The Institute for American Values published a report from family scholars in 2002 entitled "Why Marriage Matters: Twenty-one Conclusions from the Social Sciences." The following are the results of just a few studies cited in that report to help you see why permanence in marriage is such a wise choice. A copy of the complete report can be obtained through the Institute of American Values (www.americanvalues.org).

I realize that statistics can be overwhelming and sometimes get to be boring, but in this case, I think the message they deliver makes it worth wading through it all. Every parent should review these findings before plunging into divorce.

Parent-Child Relationships

The parent-child relationship is crucial to a child's happiness and success in life. But studies have shown that divorce doubles the number of children who have a poor relationship with both parents. In one study, 30 percent of the children of divorced parents reported a poor relationship with their mother, while only 16 percent of the children of parents who stay married reported a poor relationship.[1] But it's even worse for fathers: 65 percent of the children of divorced parents have a poor relationship with their father compared to 29 percent in non-divorced families.[2] And divorce has a negative effect on father-child relationships even when compared to those in an unhappy marriage.[3]

Having counseled hundreds of families going through a divorce, it's not too difficult to understand why divorce has such a negative effect on parent-child relationships. The battle between divorcing parents ultimately sucks children into the fray, and they become unwilling conscripts. Both parents seek their loyalty, and the result is usually a child's disrespect for the immature way the parents are handling things.

What a child needs is safety and security. But a divorce caused by the parents creates chaos. It's no wonder that children of divorced parents lose respect for their parents' ability to make wise decisions. Instead of going to parents for advice and direction in life, they go to their peers—the blind leading the blind.

Economic Security

Divorce also robs a child of economic security. They're not only more likely to be *raised* in poverty, but they're also more likely to *remain* in poverty or economic hardship for the rest of their lives. An intact family is one of the most impressive economic advantages for children, both while they're growing up and later on when they become adults.[4]

The economic advantage of marriage comes from more than just the combination of two incomes: married men earn about 15 percent more than single men do.[5] Their greater commitment to their work, healthier personal habits, and the emotional support of a wife are important factors in their success.[6]

The efficiency of marriage itself offers another economic advantage. As is the case with most business partnerships, a husband and wife can provide specialized skills, creating a higher quality of life for both of them with the same amount of effort. They tend to invest long-term, building equity in their home and in savings accounts. Spouses whose marriages remain intact also benefit far more from inheritance than spouses who have divorced.[7]

An important factor in the economic success of children is education. But divorce increases the likelihood that children will fail in school. Children of divorce are more likely to have lower grades, to be held back, and to drop out of high school.[8] They are less likely to graduate from college and to achieve high-status jobs and more likely to end up unemployed. This disadvantage is just as great for children whose parents remarry as it is for children living with single mothers.[9]

A mother and father who are committed in marriage make a special effort to guarantee the economic security of their offspring. And that effort produces impressive results, not only while children are growing up, but throughout their entire lives.

Health

There are also health advantages for children whose biological parents remain married, and that advantage persists long after they leave home.[10] In fact, such children not only have fewer health problems in life, but they also tend to live longer by an average of four years.[11] One study concluded that "parental divorce sets off a negative chain of events, which contribute to a higher mortality risk among individuals from divorced homes."[12]

Parents receive marriage's health advantage as well. Married people have better health[13] and live longer[14] than those who are divorced. The results of studies have shown that the health benefit of marriage is found across a wide variety of "diseases, impairments, functioning problems, and disabilities."[15]

The health advantage of marriage alone is so impressive that any couple considering divorce should realize that it will likely increase their risk of disease and decrease their lifespan. It's something that few couples consider when making that fateful decision.

It isn't just physical health that's at risk, however. Divorce also increases the risk of serious mental illness for children.[16] Children of divorced parents are also far more likely to commit suicide.[17] The rate of suicide among adolescents and young adults has tripled in the past fifty years, caused primarily by the effects of divorce on children.[18]

Parents, especially mothers, are also at a higher risk for emotional disorders. Depression and suicide are far more likely to occur among divorced men and women than those who are married.[19] And when a divorced mother becomes acutely depressed, its effect on her children is devastating. She is unable to provide the support they need, and they have less access to the healthy parent who would have provided the support if the marriage had remained intact.[20]

Crime and Violence

The sons of divorced parents are far more likely to commit crimes than boys raised by their biological parents. And when raised by a stepfather, they're even more likely to commit crimes.[21] This is one of the reasons I've advised the divorced mothers of boys to remain unmarried until their children are grown. And it's not just criminal behavior of boys that increases with divorce. Both boys and girls exhibit more deviant behavior when raised in one-parent or remarried homes than those whose parents are not divorced.[22] These children are more easily influenced by their peers than their parents, which sets the stage for delinquent behavior.[23] As I already mentioned, the children of divorced parents tend to lose respect for their parents' judgment, since they willfully made a choice that pulled the rug out from under them.

One of the most impressive benefits of permanent marriage is its safety. Violence against both men and women is four times more likely outside of marriage. And single and divorced women are ten times more likely to be raped.[24] Marriage also makes people less likely to commit violent offenses. One study found that juvenile offenders who married and stayed married were two-thirds less likely to commit a future offense.[25]

Although domestic violence remains an important problem in marriage, women are three times more likely to be the victims of domestic violence when they're not married.[26] And the most dangerous relationship for women is cohabitation, when a woman lives with a man outside of marriage.[27] This result has been found so consistently that all women should know by now that cohabitation is extremely dangerous and makes absolutely no sense. Yet the rate of cohabitation, and the domestic abuse that follows, is increasing each year.

Children are also at greater risk of violence and abuse *after* a divorce, especially when their mother remarries. The risk of sexual abuse of preschool girls by a stepfather is forty times greater than it is when they live with their biological parents.[28] And the boyfriends of single mothers have been found to commit half of all reported child abuse by nonparents.[29]

These and other studies make it clear that divorce carries with it very negative consequences to children. Any parent who cares for the happiness and success of his or her children should avoid divorce at almost all costs. There are very few reasons for divorce that justify the damage it does to children.

In the next chapter, I will take a close look at the reasons most people give for their divorce. Are some justified? I would say "yes." Quite frankly, in spite of the negative consequences of divorce on children, I've actually recommended divorce to clients under certain conditions.

But our laws have blurred the distinction between good reasons for divorce and trivial reasons. They've done that through the creation of the "no-fault" divorce. In spite of the fact that the marriage contract is one of our most important social agreements and that breaking it can have devastating social consequences, our laws have blinded us to reasons that really *do* justify divorce. And when the reasons are unjustified, these laws fail to guide couples toward solutions to marital problems that would save marriages and protect children.

11

Is "No-Fault" at Fault?

Laws That Encourage Divorce

From 1935 up to the present, state legislatures and state supreme courts have quietly been enacting laws that encourage infidelity. In most cases, witnesses were never given a chance to oppose the change. For that matter, witnesses didn't even testify to support the change. And as we've already seen in part 2 of this book, the legal rationale for change was seriously flawed. But in spite of these and other serious problems, legislators and jurists alike enthusiastically enacted laws that did away with penalties for infidelity, and no one seemed to care. Today, only eight states remain committed to fidelity in marriage (see chapter 8).

The same thing can be said for laws that encourage divorce. Most states had already abandoned legal constraints against divorce by 1974, and by 1985 all fifty states had made the marriage contract so trivial that they did not even require a justifiable reason for divorce. And once again, it was all done under the radar screen. Marriage is now one of the only legal contracts that is non-binding. And the laws making it all possible were passed with very little public awareness or debate.

Without a doubt, the liberalization of laws against infidelity and divorce has undermined traditional marriage and has crippled families for the past thirty years. Along with high divorce rates, we now see our entire society drifting into two classes of people: those who were raised by their natural parents who remain married for life and those who were not. One group tends to be healthy, economically secure, and productive, while the other group tends to struggle.

When these laws were first passed, most legal experts and social scientists could not have known the tragedy that would follow. They didn't know that the children of divorced parents would suffer serious disadvantages and that those disadvantages would lead to educational, economic, physical, and mental health problems that would follow them throughout life. In fact, as I said before, some of the "experts" at the time claimed that divorce would be good for these children.

We now know better. Divorce is not only a tragedy for children, but it's also a tragedy for those who divorce. As we saw in the last chapter, divorce leaves parents disadvantaged in many of the same ways as it does their children. And because divorce creates such serious problems for parents and children alike, it's a problem for our society in general.

In other words, the value of the marriage contract goes beyond the interests of a husband and wife. It's valuable to their children, to the extended members of their family, and to all of society. That's why the marriage vow is made before "God and witnesses." It's a serious agreement that has far-reaching consequences. Government has an obligation to support all contracts, but this one is among the most important for government to support because it affects all of us. So how were laws guarding permanence in marriage so easily eliminated?

A Modern Disaster

It's difficult to explain how laws that abandoned the family were enacted. And you may find my explanation a little hard to follow. But if you stick with me, you'll witness the unfolding of one of our greatest modern disasters.

Let's begin this excursion by looking back at divorce law as it existed prior to 1965. In most states, adultery was a valid reason for divorce because the marriage agreement itself promised fidelity for life, and an affair is obviously a gross violation of those terms. The betrayed spouse was granted the right to end the marriage with divorce, and there were serious consequences for the offending spouse. He or she usually suffered serious financial and custodial penalties for being the cause of the divorce. Such laws not only made a clear public statement that infidelity was wrong, but they also helped compensate the betrayed spouses and children who were damaged by such behavior.

Today, of course, things have changed. The spouse having the affair can now be the one to file for divorce, and he or she may suffer absolutely no penalty. Betrayed spouses, who have done nothing to violate their marital agreement, can now find themselves divorced, stripped of half of their assets, having lost custody of their children, and in some cases, financially responsible for their unfaithful ex-spouse. That's the law.

In 1965, New York, like most other states, accepted adultery as a legitimate cause for divorce. But what made

New York different was that adultery was the only cause that the state would accept. And divorce was allowed only if adultery could be proven. So as you might imagine, spouses wanting a divorce badly enough would trump up false charges of adultery to get the job done. They would even hire professional perjurers to testify on the witness stand that their faithful spouse was seen in bed with someone else. Many women in New York at the time made a very good living lying under oath that they were having affairs with innocent husbands.

Perjury was not the only way to get around the divorce law in New York, however. New York residents could also divorce in Nevada if they established residency there for just six weeks. Take a six-week Nevada vacation, and return to New York divorced. That's how the wife of Governor Nelson Rockefeller obtained her divorce in 1962.

Since it was rather easy to hire professional perjurers or to skirt New York divorce laws by simply leaving the state for a few weeks, some argued that the integrity of the state's entire legal system was at stake. They could have solved the problem by cracking down on the perjury industry with laws that penalized perjurers with stiff penalties, making it too risky to attempt for the amount of money they were paid. And they could have passed a law, or even a state constitutional amendment, that refused to recognize divorce that was granted in any other state.

But they didn't do that. Instead, they liberalized their divorce laws.

Grounds for divorce were expanded to include not just adultery but also cruel and inhuman treatment, abandonment for two or more years, and confinement in a prison for three or more years. If those had been the only changes made, New York would have simply joined most other states in providing several more causes for divorce, all of them reasonable.

178

But they added one other cause to the list—an agreed-upon separation of two years. In other words, if a husband and wife agreed to separate for two years, they needed no reason to divorce. It would be granted by the state at their request. To make this new "cause" more palatable to conservatives and Catholics, counseling for possible reconciliation was mandatory during those two years.[1] These new standards passed with very little opposition in April 1966.

This was just the beginning. Within four years, New York legislators had reduced the separation period from two years to only one year, and three years after that, conciliation counseling during that time was abandoned. A one-year, agreed-upon separation was all that spouses needed to be granted a divorce. No cause was required, and no effort was made to keep the family together. New York had, in effect, become a no-fault divorce state, though no one thought of it in those terms at the time.

But New York wasn't the only state that had enacted no-fault-like provisions in its divorce law. Arkansas passed a law in 1937 that allowed divorce after a separation of three years.[2] In 1953 Oklahoma included "incompatibility" as grounds for divorce.[3] And in 1957 Texas permitted separation as a cause for divorce.[4] It's not surprising that these states have some of the highest divorce rates of any states in the country today.

No-Fault Becomes Official

The state that actually brought no-fault divorce out into the open was California. As was the case with New York, it was done with very little opposition. During the 1960s the divorce law in California was already among the most lenient. All that was needed was proof of "cruelty," which could be as benign as an occasional disrespectful remark. Since all couples fail in that regard from time to time, any spouse wanting a divorce could prove that a spouse was "cruel" to satisfy the law. I counseled scores of California couples during those years, and I know from firsthand experience how trivial the complaints usually were and how easy it was to divorce using those complaints as proof of cruelty.

Even before no-fault laws were officially enacted, a wife wanting a divorce in California would simply tell me that she had fallen out of love with her husband. She would admit that her husband's greatest fault was that he'd become boring and that she didn't want to live with a boring man. While I was always shocked to hear that a mother would be willing to gamble the future of her children's lives away for lack of love, few of the women I counseled were at all defensive about the reason for their decision.

In June 1966, those who wanted to eliminate causes for divorce in California got an unexpected, and very welcome, ally to their cause—the Archbishop of Canterbury, world leader of the Anglican (Episcopal) Church. In his report on divorce, *Putting Asunder*, he suggested eliminating all existing grounds for divorce and replacing them with "marital breakdown." That action would pave the way for a relatively painless divorce.[5]

A month earlier, in May 1966, Governor Edmund Brown had appointed the Governor's Commission on the Family. One of the commission's goals was to "study and suggest revision, where necessary, of the substantive laws of California relating to the family." It held no public hearings and issued no press releases until the final report was completed. Since Brown lost to conservative Ronald Reagan in his bid for a third term that fall, the commission rushed completion of the report to be delivered to Brown just two weeks before he left office. That report was the first official proposal for no-fault divorce law in California.

While the report was written to convey a pro-family impression, "to further the stability of the family," it focused its primary effort and attention on eliminating legal grounds for divorce. Quoting extensively from the Archbishop of Canterbury's report, it insisted that it was in the best interest of society and marriage itself to rewrite divorce laws. To get a taste of its optimism regarding judicial review and the social sciences coming to the defense of marriage, read the following excerpt from what the commission wrote about the proposed no-fault law:

> We cannot overemphasize that this standard does not permit divorce by consent, wherein marriage is treated as wholly a private contract terminable at the pleasure of the parties without any effective intervention by society. The standard we propose requires the community to assert its interest in the status of the family, and permits dissolution of the marriage only after it has been subjected to a penetrating scrutiny and the judicial process has provided the parties with all of the resources of social science in aid of conciliation.[6]

The recommendations made by the committee sounded pretty good with this family-friendly language. After all, it made sense that discerning judges and competent mediators could intervene in marital disputes and help save marriages headed for divorce. Without that promise of intervention, no-fault divorce law might have been seen for what it really was—a knife in the heart of traditional marriage.

No One's Fault

Chief among the committee's recommendations was eliminating all fault grounds for divorce and replacing

181

them with the requirement that the marriage be declared in a state of "irreparable breakdown." As we've already seen, the committee appeared supportive of marriage, insisting that judges would have a high standard for what they would consider "irreparable." It also insisted that social science would be able to find ways to repair the bulk of marriages that were strained but not in an "irreparable" state.

If the committee had taken the time to ask judges and social scientists if they felt qualified to assume such responsibility for evaluating and repairing marriages, they would have encountered an immediate problem. Judges did not want to decide the reparability of a marriage, and social scientists were acutely aware of how expensive and relatively ineffective marital therapy was at the time. Sadly, social science is still ineffective in saving marriages. A 1995 *Consumer Report* survey found that marital therapy received the lowest rating when compared to all other forms of psychotherapy.[7]

Actually, very few social scientists I knew at the time were even suggesting that couples *should* remain married if they had conflicts. Instead they were encouraging couples to divorce, claiming that they had simply married the wrong person. Of course, many of these counselors had been divorced themselves, so it's no wonder they didn't have much faith in the idea of reconciling couples with marital problems.

New Language Levels the Field

In addition to eliminating all fault grounds for divorce, the committee made other recommendations as well. Among them was the recommendation to change the language in divorce litigation. For example, instead of "Brown v. Brown," the case for divorce between a Mr. and Mrs. Brown was to be referred to as "In re: the marriage of Browns." Instead of a "complaint," a "petition of inquiry" was filed to initiate the court action. And the term "divorce" was to be replaced by "marital dissolution."

It was further suggested that property be distributed equally, rather than by fault. Up until this point, a spouse who was physically violent or had been unfaithful could lose all or part of his or her portion of the couple's property to the innocent spouse. With this change to eliminate fault from the process, there would be no penalty for bad behavior. And without fault in the equation, child custody would be held jointly rather than given to one parent or the other.

Because prominent Catholic laymen were part of the commission, and because the commission painted a pro-family perspective, it managed to escape close scrutiny by California's Catholic leadership. And conservative Governor Ronald Reagan had his hands full trying to cut the California budget, dealing with growing protests over the Vietnam War, and facing pressure to enact abortion legislation. In addition, Reagan was divorced himself. So careful scrutiny of the commission's report didn't come out of the governor's office either. (I think it's worthy to note that the Republican governors of both New York and California were divorced when laws were passed eliminating cause for divorce.)

No-Fault Stands, Saving Marriages Falls

The proposals of the Governor's Commission on the Family were first introduced to the California legislature in 1967. Yet even with the recommendation of the California Bar Association, it took two years before they were finally written into law. During those two years, legislators all had an opportunity to become familiar with these new and radical concepts, couched in pro-family terms.

A Republican member of the commission, Donald Grunsky, was the principle sponsor of the bill. At the heart of his proposal was the new family court system that would use special counseling and judicial scrutiny to prevent a spouse from divorcing for frivolous reasons, such as the temporary loss of love. But when the idea of a family court system was debated, two obstacles to this new system immediately came to the forefront. First, California was trying to cut the budget at the time, and aside from the fact that social science didn't know how to save marriages, the cost of trying to do so would have been gigantic. Second, judges were alarmed to hear that they would be asked to decide whether or not a marriage was potentially repairable. They wanted absolutely no part of that responsibility. As a result, the new family court system was completely abandoned, and along with it, any hope of using the new no-fault provision to try to save marriages was also abandoned.

Grunsky should have seen what was happening. He was aware of the fact that no-fault divorce law made sense from a pro-family perspective only if the family court system existed. So he should have encouraged his conservative colleagues to reject the entire concept of no-fault divorce if it was not to be accompanied by the proposed family court system.

Instead, Grunsky took his bill off the table and passed the torch to James Hayes, another legislator, who sponsored an alternative bill. Hayes himself was facing a divorce at the time, and it gave him an opportunity to write rules that were in his favor. His bill contained the committee's recommendations for no-fault provisions but *without* the family court system. It was passed by both houses of the legislature and signed by then-Governor Reagan in June 1969.

With that, California became the first no-fault divorce state. From that day forward, any resident of California could be granted a divorce for undefined "irreconcilable differences." Divorce petitions themselves contained the vocabulary suggested by the commission. And equal division of property with alimony to be paid temporarily rather than permanently (as had been the case) became the norm.[8]

Let me summarize what happened in California. In 1966, the Governor's Commission on the Family recommended eliminating fault as grounds for divorce. What had made the commission's report seem reasonable, especially to Catholics and to Republicans who were on the committee, was its emphasis on a new family court system that would help struggling couples reconcile. By leaving fault out of the legal process of divorce, proponents argued, couples would have an easier time reconciling, which would ultimately make families more stable. Judges were to use very conservative critera before they would agree that a couple truly had irreconcilable differences, so it was hoped that the rate of divorce would decrease.

But it was all a smoke screen. When the bill finally got to the floor of the legislature in 1969, the new family court system had been summarily dismissed. It's likely that many of those on the commission knew that counseling would be too expensive for the state and that judges wouldn't want to decide which marriages were irreconcilable. But they were able to pull the wool over the eyes of their naïve colleagues, who never went to the trouble of asking judges or social scientists what they thought of the idea. In the end, California had enacted a law that allowed couples to break a contract that is at the very heart of our society—without any justifiable reason.

No-Fault Divorce Law Spreads to the Nation

No-fault divorce law was attractive to legislators because existing law was so unattractive. Where state divorce law required cause, a divorcing spouse would often fabricate cause, ruining the reputation of an innocent spouse. Where state law required a cooling-off period of one or two years, a spouse would simply live in Nevada for six weeks to be granted a divorce.

Anyone who has witnessed a divorce hearing that tries to establish cause knows that the emotional reactions of everyone involved are usually over-the-top. It can't possibly be healthy. In many cases a husband, wife, and the children are each represented by their own attorneys, each trying uncompromisingly to be awarded the very best outcome for their client. That not only makes compromise almost impossible, but it usually costs far more than most families can afford. So the cause-based system seemed to encourage conflict in a situation crying for conciliation. A nonadversarial alternative to cause-based divorce seemed to be the answer to this vexing problem.

There was also the problem of disparity of law. Every state seemed to have its own rules for divorce. And within some states, even counties could have their own unique rules. So it made sense for divorce reformers to try to create laws that would make divorce less adversarial, and then make those laws standard in every state throughout the country.

The National Conference of Commissioners on Uniform State Laws (NCCUSL) took the lead in this effort. Founded in 1892, its members are legal experts who are appointed by state governors. Its purpose, as its name suggests, is to help make state laws more uniform. Proposals from this group are sent to the American Bar Association (ABA). When both groups stand together on a proposal, it carries considerable weight with state legislators.

The effort of the NCCUSL to draft a Uniform Marriage and Divorce Act (UMDA) began in 1967, before California's no-fault divorce law had been enacted. But the appointment of California's Herma Hill Kay to provide the committee with drafts and supporting material helped keep the committee aware of her state's formulation of the no-fault law. And Kay had been a very influential voice in that law's development.

There were no public hearings or media coverage during the drafting of the UMDA. Very few special interest groups even knew about it. Leaders of the Catholic Church were almost entirely in the dark. But then so were the feminist organizations that would have supported it.

In 1969 as the committee was debating its proposal, paragraph by paragraph, California's new no-fault divorce law was enacted. It pulled the rug out from under those who were arguing that such a proposal wasn't practical and could never be enacted because of the opposition of conservatives and Catholics. California's new law proved that neither of those groups would stand in its way.

As was the case with the development of the California law, the motive for strengthening families was originally an essential ingredient to keep members of the committee thinking that no-fault divorce law was for the good of the family. But in the end, when it came time to implement the necessary precautions to protect marriage, the true motive became clear. The NCCUSL rejected Kay's family court proposal, just as the California legislature had rejected it. In fact, the final proposal didn't even mention conciliation.

When the UMDA was sent to the ABA for its approval in 1970, its failure to deal even superficially with the protection of families got it into deep trouble. Henry Foster, chair of the ABA's Family Law Section, correctly observed that the UMDA would lead to "administrative divorce upon request." It offered no protection for the other spouse from a divorce being granted for frivolous reasons.[9] Foster saw it for what it really was—a law that allowed the breaking of a valuable contract for no just reason.

More Laws in the Making

If all of this law history hasn't totally confused you or put you to sleep but instead has left you wanting even more, I encourage you to read *Silent Revolution: The Transformation of Divorce Law in the United States* (University of Chicago Press, 1988) by Herbert Jacob. Much of the information I've presented here comes from Jacob's excellent synopsis of events.

By 1974, however, the Family Law Section of the ABA had eventually agreed to the UMDA with minor changes, none of them having to do with conciliation. Instead, a ninety-day waiting period was recommended so that no one would have to go to the expense of staying in Nevada for six weeks to obtain a divorce. Again, it was a change that actually encouraged divorce rather than reconciliation.

With the endorsement of the NCCUSL and the ABA, the UMDA was presented to state legislatures throughout the country. Many states adopted no-fault law easily—without any legislative debate or ruling of their supreme courts. Instead, in 1974 and in later updates, they were simply listed in the journal of the Family Law Section of the *Family Law Quarterly* as no-fault divorce states.[10] Eventually, a majority of the states adopted no-fault divorce provisions by being added to this list. This radical change in family law was accepted in most states without so much as a single public hearing.

By 1974 forty-five states had enacted some elements of no-fault divorce law. And by 1985 the last holdout, South Dakota, finally joined the others. But only fifteen of the fifty states actually eliminated all fault provisions from their divorce law.[11] The other states gave couples a choice between no-fault and fault grounds for divorce. In these states, if one spouse objected to the vague cause, "irretrievable breakdown," fault such as adultery or cruelty would have to be established. In twenty states separation by either spouse for as short as six months (Vermont) or as long as five years (Rhode Island) was acceptable cause for divorce.

One of His Worst Mistakes Ever

No-fault laws in California began a wave of legal changes in divorce law that had far-reaching consequences. At the time it happened, then-Governor Reagan was preoccupied with other pressing issues and didn't imagine the negative impact that new law would have on families. But in his book *Twice Adopted*, Michael Reagan, son of Ronald Reagan and a victim of his father's divorce, describes his father's role in creating California's no-fault divorce law and that law's tragic consequences. He writes,

> Dad later said that he regretted signing the no-fault divorce bill and that he believed it was one of the worst mistakes he ever made in office. That law set in motion one of the most damaging social experiments in the history of our nation. Not only did the divorce rate skyrocket as a direct result of the no-fault experiment, but divorce conflicts and legal costs remain as ruinous as ever. The acrimony in divorce has simply shifted to different issues. Instead of fighting over who gets blamed for what, couples battle primarily over custody, visitation rights, and child support.[12]

As someone with firsthand experience with the fallout from divorce, Reagan quotes Judy Parejko to express some of his own reactions to the effects of divorce on a child. "Divorce is where two adults take everything that matters to a child—the child's home, family, security, and sense of being loved and protected—and they smash it all up, leave it in ruins on the floor, then walk out and leave the child to clean up the mess."[13]

189

So what does Michael Reagan suggest to *prevent* children from being damaged by divorce? "Don't get divorced!"

Precisely.

There's no acceptable substitute for the nurturing that a biological mother and father are capable of providing to their children. But it has become far too easy for a couple who are temporarily out of love to throw in the towel. A turnaround can take as long as two years for couples who find themselves at odds with each other. At a moment in time, they can think that there's no hope. But an injection of the extraordinary care that I described earlier in this book is all that it takes to turn potential tragedy into marital bliss.

At the time of crisis, some couples will tell me that the only reason they are staying together is for their children. I tell them that that *is* reason enough because divorce, the alternative, is about the worst thing parents can do to their children. But they don't have to settle for just "staying together." The best thing parents can do for their children is to show each other the extraordinary care that was promised at the wedding. And that care will restore their love for each other. As long as they're going to be together for the sake of their children, why not have a terrific marriage—for the sake of the children and each other?

12

How to Divorce-Proof Your Marriage

Overcoming Cultural and Legal
Obstacles to Permanence

You face an uphill battle if you are trying to make your marriage permanent. Few these days would agree with me that permanence should be one of the primary goals of *every* marriage. And fewer still would agree with what it takes to *guarantee* permanence in marriage—extraordinary care. Most of the books and articles written about marriage downplay the importance of meeting intimate emotional needs, ridicule couples who make an effort to avoid the Love Busters we've talked about in this book, and express downright horror at the notion that a married couple should make all of their decisions with each other in mind.

You won't get much help from our laws, either. If you or your spouse ever decide to make a run for it, our laws and the social services that enforce them will be right there to encourage a speedy divorce. There will be very little to prevent you from making the biggest mistake of your life.

Incentives to Divorce

I remember counseling couples in the early 1970s who came to me with a profound dilemma. They loved each other and wanted to stay married for life, but they were being offered high incentives to end their marriage. An apartment, healthcare, legal services, food, clothing, and a substantial cash allowance were being offered to them by our state's social services agency on the condition that they divorce. Faced with the financial stress that most young couples face, it was a tempting offer.

What? you may ask. *Why would the state deliberately encourage couples to divorce?*

Of course, welfare workers were not actually *telling* people to divorce. But they were telling married couples that they did not qualify for substantial welfare benefits. Only those who were unmarried or in the process of divorcing need apply. And many couples who were struggling to pay their bills got the message. Stay married and expect no government assistance. Be divorced and the government will help provide the financial assistance you needed for food, housing, healthcare, etc.

Some couples thought the answer might be to divorce but remain lovers secretly. I counseled against such action—an increase in income from the government did *not* justify a breakdown of their family. But most of them didn't take my advice.

Years later I found myself counseling some of the daughters of these couples—this time because these girls had learned that if they had a child out of wedlock, they would get the same generous support from the government. Imagine offering a fourteen-year-old the equivalent of roughly $2,500 per month in 1980s dollars if she would simply have a child. It seemed like winning the lottery!

These teenage girls didn't need to attend school, and they didn't even need to find a job. All they needed for financial security and independence was to find someone to get them pregnant. Their job for life would then be raising their own children. And the more children they had, the more money they would receive in benefits, as long as they didn't marry the father of those children.

The boyfriends in these cases also learned that marriage had become obsolete, so they didn't need to do what it took to support a family. The government would support their family as long as they didn't marry. Therefore, they didn't need to complete school, and they didn't need to develop a career. Their girlfriends were no longer looking for men who could support them. All they needed was someone who could show them a good time, which often included providing them with mood-altering drugs. It was a formula for poverty and crime.

As I watched this tragedy unfold, I could see where it would lead. The poor would no longer have any incentive to become educated to help bring them out of poverty. They would no longer want to create careers to help bring them out of poverty. And they would no longer marry to help bring them out of poverty.

I believe that one of the most important causes for the poor remaining poor was our government's ill-advised

Is Money the Root of Most Divorces?

Some have argued that financial problems are the number one cause of divorce. They're wrong. Divorce is the number one cause of financial problems for those who were once married. And for those who are single, marriage is one of the most certain paths out of poverty, especially when the marriage is between the biological parents of children.

welfare program. Marriage had not only encouraged men to educate themselves and to develop their careers so that they could support their families, but it had also provided the necessary stability that people needed to escape poverty. But the welfare program offered strong incentives to avoid marriage. And no-fault divorce law made it easy for married couples to change their marital status to take advantage of the system.

In truth, our government was only following advice given by many leading social scientists who felt that marriage had become obsolete. Although they had no evidence to support it, they believed that marriage forced women and children to be trapped into a dangerous environment, and that the sooner they could be independent of men, the better.

Some of these people, mostly feminists, are still around, but they're a lot less vocal now that we have incontrovertible evidence that marriage is the very *safest* environment for women and children. It's actually the alternatives to marriage that are unsafe. But it took a generation of meltdown among poor families for most social scientists to figure that out (see chapter 10).

Thankfully, things are now changing. Our government has learned its lesson. Instead of offering lavish financial incentives for those who divorce or bear children out of wedlock, it now offers only limited help while a mother is being trained to eventually support herself and her children without government help. Since most women don't relish the idea of raising children as a working single mother, an increasing number of young mothers are now looking to men they will marry instead of to government for their support. And instead of being valued for only their ability to entertain and provide drugs, those young men are beginning to be valued for their education and career development.

Marriage has now become a viable alternative again for young men and women. Our government has even come to recognize that marriage is one of the most important ways to overcome poverty and crime.

Is It Too Late?

Has too much damage already been done? Is it realistic to assume that a generation of marital failure will reverse itself and create a new generation of successful marriages? Few of those who have been the beneficiaries of past welfare benefits know what it's like to be in a permanent relationship.

And it isn't just the poor who are ignorant. Our entire culture has been teaching us so many lies about marriage that there are very few left who still have a healthy understanding. Instead of knowing how to maintain a permanent romantic relationship in marriage, most men and women have experienced years of failure, going from one romantic relationship to another. And they've passed their ignorance on to their children.

As we saw in chapter 6, Michael Gurian and other like-minded social philosophers believe that romance inevitably leads to disillusionment. They don't equate romance with permanence—they equate it with an almost inevitable breakup. They feel that the only way to make marriages permanent is to stop trying to make them romantic. Instead of teaching those in the next generation what it takes to have a permanent romantic relationship in marriage, they teach them that it's not possible.

So in spite of the fact that a permanent marriage has now been shown to be an advantage to everyone, both rich and poor, there are very few who have experienced a permanently romantic marriage themselves. And there are even fewer who can teach us how to have a permanent marriage.

Why do so many people in our culture believe that a romantic relationship in marriage cannot be permanent? Joyce and I are not unique. There are millions of couples just like us who have been in love for decades. Granted, we're in the minority. Only about one couple in five have had this experience. But the fact that we exist proves conclusively that it's not impossible. Yet there are a host of people who don't want to believe it. Why?

Buyers, Renters, and Freeloaders

To help you understand why some people cling to the assumption that a permanent romantic relationship is impossible, I'd like to introduce you to three dominant belief systems regarding romantic relationships. I present them to you in the form of an analogy to help me explain how each of these determines the future of a relationship—a happy marriage or an inevitable breakup. And they will also help me explain why there are so many who refuse to believe that a permanent romantic relationship is possible.

Imagine your relationship as if it were a house, and consider the following three types of inhabitants who could live at that house:

Freeloaders are like those who live in a house without paying rent or doing anything to improve it unless they're in the mood to do so. They do not believe that much effort should go into the care of a partner in a romantic relationship. Either the relationship is or it isn't meant to be. They agree to do only what comes naturally and expect only what comes naturally. In their opinion, doing more than that only serves to prolong an incompatible relationship. They do not believe in extraordinary care.

196

Renters are like those who rent a house and are willing to stay as long as the conditions seem fair, or until they find something better. And they argue with the manager to try to improve a steadily decaying residence or to pay less rent. These folks believe that the amount and quality of care given in a romantic relationship should be fair, and they keep score regularly. If what they give isn't judged by them to be proportional to what they take, they either decrease what they give or demand more of what they take. This leads to a steady decrease of care for each other, since most people view what they give as being of greater value than what they take. It also leads to fights that try to force each other to give more. Renters are notoriously abusive and controlling, and their solutions to problems are usually short-term solutions since their commitment is not long-term. Sacrifices are expected because there is little empathy for the interests and feelings of the other partner, as is the case with tenants and landlords. They provide more care than Freeloaders in a romantic relationship. But their care is not extraordinary.

Buyers, on the other hand, are like those who buy a house for life with a willingness to make repairs that accommodate changing needs—painting the walls, installing a new carpet, replacing the roof, and even doing some remodeling—so that it can be comfortable and useful to them. They make a long-term investment in a romantic relationship because they view that commitment to be exclusive and permanent. They regard their care for their partner to be as important as their care for themselves. When they meet their spouse's emotional needs, they do it as if they were meeting their own needs. When they make decisions, they consult their partner first, because they view their partner's feelings as if they

197

were their own. Permanent changes in their behavior and lifestyle that make the relationship mutually fulfilling make more sense to them than short-term changes that are good for one and bad for the other. Sacrifices are not expected or tolerated—they look for win-win solutions to problems. Buyers provide extraordinary care in a romantic relationship.

If you cling to the beliefs of a Freeloader or Renter, then it's clearly impossible to maintain a long-term romantic relationship. As a Freeloader, your romantic relationship would end at the first sighting of adversity. And as a Renter, your romantic relationship would always eventually turn to disillusion, followed by abuse and control. It's only when you think like a Buyer that it's possible to have a romantic relationship that lasts permanently.

It's not uncommon for most happily married couples to have worked their way up from Freeloaders to Renters while they were dating and finally to Buyers when they married. That's how my wife, Joyce, and I developed our relationship. There's nothing wrong with being a Freeloader in the first stages of a romantic relationship or being a Renter when the relationship looks promising.

The problem arises when partners do not eventually become Buyers. That's because Freeloaders and Renters are not willing to provide the extraordinary care that a lasting romantic relationship requires, and as a result, they make very disappointing marriage partners—the romantic part of their relationship inevitably disappears. Only Buyers can create a permanent romantic relationship that keeps marriage passionate and mutually fulfilling because they continue to provide the extraordinary care essential to a lasting relationship.

Of course Freeloaders and Renters can become Buyers. All it takes is a willingness to provide extraordinary care consistently and permanently. Even if a couple has had a very bad marriage, they can have a lifetime of passion together if they simply stop freeloading or renting and start buying.

Anti-Buyer Culture

My experience counseling California couples in the late 1960s introduced me to the challenge that would face marriage counselors for the next century and beyond: When these people married, they tended not to become Buyers. They remained Freeloaders and Renters. When they married, they did not view marriage as a commitment to provide extraordinary care. Instead, they saw it as a relationship that required very little care, as in the case of Freeloaders, or a relationship that required as little care as possible, as in the case of Renters.

Don't get me wrong. These people were in love when they first married, and they married because of their love for each other. But they didn't understand the importance of extraordinary care in marriage. And that lack of understanding prevented them from maintaining their love for each other.

Freeloaders lost their love for each other the quickest—usually in the first few months of marriage—because they did the least to provide care in marriage. And Renters lost their love next, because their quality of care for each other tended to decrease over time. When they thought their spouse was not caring enough for them, they showed less care themselves. Eventually, neither of them was caring for each other. Instead, they argued about the care they thought they deserved.

At first I couldn't understand why married couples were not all Buyers. When a spouse told me that the marriage was not worth saving because it had lost its passion, I was confused. *There are more reasons to be married than just passion*, I thought. I tried to persuade couples that we have an obligation to provide extraordinary care in marriage, especially when life is tough. It's a promise to be kept in joy or sorrow, in plenty or want, in health or sickness. What good is the promise of care if it's kept only when life is terrific!

I also used religious reasons. The wedding vow was not only made to a spouse, it was also made to God. At the time of the wedding we promise God that we will care for our spouse for life. Since many of those I counseled were Christians, I showed them verses from the Bible that state unequivocally that divorce is a sin against God. If they wanted to please God and live according to his purposes, they could not divorce their spouse.

Then there were also a host of practical reasons to stay married. I tried to convince couples that a permanent marriage was of crucial importance to their children and to themselves. There was some research, even back in the 1960s, that showed married couples to be happier, healthier, and wealthier than those who divorced.

I used ethical, religious, and practical reasons to try to keep couples together. But these were reasons that only a Buyer would understand. And I was talking to Freeloaders and Renters. So every time I encouraged a couple to stay married using the logic and reasoning of a Buyer, the couple divorced.

I even tried to change my strategy to conform to the popular approach of the day—communication training. If a couple were to improve their communication with each other, I reasoned, they would want to provide extraordinary care to each other and stay married. I received special training to teach couples how to communicate with understanding and respect for each other's opinions.

That didn't work either. Some of the most articulate people I counseled—experts at speaking respectfully and listening with excellent comprehension—divorced. They didn't want to care for each other, and no amount of communication training could change that fact. Ironically, the marriage expert who trained me to teach couples to communicate was eventually divorced.

But the communication training taught me a valuable lesson. The reason I was failing to save marriages is that I wasn't listening. Freeloaders and Renters were telling me why they chose to make that decision, and I was not accepting it because I was a Buyer. I had to begin thinking as a Freeloader or Renter if I were to save their marriages.

Couples were telling me that they were not committed to a lifetime of extraordinary care. In fact, they weren't committed to care at all! They had lost their feeling of love because they had not received the care they needed from each other. And yet they were not willing to provide that care themselves.

I also made another valuable observation. I found that even when Renters and Freeloaders were married to someone who was unfaithful, abusive, or addicted, or someone who had abandoned them, if they were still in love, they didn't want to divorce. I counseled many who should have divorced because their spouses were too irresponsible or dangerous to be around. Yet I could not convince them that they should end their marriage. Instead, they wanted me to help their spouses overcome their irresponsibility and violent behavior.

Those observations led me to one of my most important insights: The best way to save the marriage of a Freeloader or Renter is to teach them how to fall in love with each other again. Then, after they were in love with each other, I could convert them into becoming Buyers. And once they became Buyers, their love for each other would remain permanent.

When dealing with Freeloaders and Renters, I found that I had to begin with the hope of restoring love rather than with the importance of marital permanence. For these people, if their relationship didn't make emotional sense, they would divorce. Once I decided to stop fighting their philosophy and start working with it instead, I started saving their marriages.

So I went to work learning how to create the feeling of love in anyone, including Renters and Freeloaders. I learned that all three aspects of extraordinary care (meeting emotional needs, avoiding Love Busters, and creating a mutually enjoyable lifestyle) contributed to the feeling of love. But it was the meeting of intimate emotional needs (intimate conversation, recreational companionship, affection, and sexual fulfillment) that had the greatest effect.

The people I counseled, especially the Renters, were willing to try out my recommendations on a short-term basis. But it didn't take long before they were able to see how extraordinary care restored their feeling of love. In spite of their beliefs regarding relationships, they were able to restore passion to their marriages by caring for each other.

I'm a Buyer. I believe that marriage is for life, and I care for my wife, Joyce, because I consider her to be a part of me. But most spouses considering divorce today are not Buyers. They care as long as it's in their best interest to care (Renters) or as long as they feel like it (Freeloaders). If counselors are to save these marriages, they must first restore their feeling of love for each other and then show them how to become Buyers.

What Is Your Commitment?

Quite frankly, I don't just defend marriage for life. I defend extraordinary care for life in marriage. If a couple is committed to the permanence of marriage without being committed to extraordinary care, they make life miserable for each other.

The traditional meaning of marriage begins with extraordinary care, and not with permanence, for a very good reason. If a couple give each other the extraordinary care they promised, permanence, which is part of the traditional meaning of marriage, is rarely an issue. It's only when extraordinary care is lacking that divorce seems reasonable.

Are you a Buyer? Is your spouse a Buyer? Or are you Renters or Freeloaders? There are several ways to guess, but the way to know for sure is to consider what would happen if you were to fall out of love with each other. A Buyer would continue to show extraordinary care in marriage even when feelings of passion have temporarily diminished or even disappeared. In other words, when Buyers marry, they are committed to extraordinary care for life, even when their feeling of love disappears and their spouse does not reciprocate.

But Renters or Freeloaders don't tend to provide extraordinary care, even when they're in love. That's why they lose their love for each other so quickly. And when they lose their feeling of love, they provide even less care for each other. The feeling of love is what motivated them to marry, and the loss of that feeling motivates them to divorce.

Granted, there are some Renters and Freeloaders who remain married after they've lost their feeling of love. But they don't provide much care for their spouse when that happens. Instead, they have an affair so they can have the advantages of marriage *and* the advantages of a romantic relationship—with two different people. Or, they may decide to live independently while married.

With about 45 percent of marriages ending in divorce and another 20 percent ending in permanent separation, the promise to "love and cherish until death do you part" isn't holding up very well. That's because our culture has produced many more Renters and Freeloaders than Buyers. If your spouse falls out of love with you, he or she is likely to join the majority of spouses and either divorce you, have an affair, or remain emotionally independent of you.

If your spouse *is* in love with you, however, you're usually safe from those outcomes—at least for the time being. And your spouse is in a good position to be converted into a Buyer if there's evidence that he or she has been a Renter or Freeloader. That's because it's much easier to justify extraordinary care when you're in love. And when you both provide it to each other, you'll stay in love.

(To learn more about Buyers, Renters, and Freeloaders, read my book *The One: A Field Guide to Relationships That Last* [Grand Rapids: Revell, 2004].)

Permanence in Marriage Requires Extraordinary Care

Odds are that you'll eventually divorce or you'll be separated by the time of your death. That's what happens to most marriages because our laws and culture encourage it. But your marriage can be the exception. You can resist the influence of our culture that encourages the beliefs of Freeloaders and Renters.

As I have already mentioned, marriage doesn't make much sense if a husband and wife do not care for each other in an extraordinary way. But divorce doesn't make sense if they provide that level of care. So when I help couples avoid divorce, I don't try to keep them together using the logic and reasoning of a Buyer, because they're Renters and Freeloaders. Instead, I teach them how to meet each other's emotional needs, avoid hurting each other, and learn how to create a mutually enjoyable lifestyle as a temporary solution to their marital problems. When they learn to provide those elements of extraordinary care, they restore their love for each other, and the risk of divorce is completely eliminated. By that time, they have plenty of evidence that the assumptions they've used as Freeloaders and Renters are seriously flawed. They see the wisdom in becoming a Buyer.

As you learn to give each other extraordinary care, you too may be fighting the Freeloader's or Renter's beliefs. You may not see how your extraordinary care can be justified. But even if you're a Freeloader or a Renter, if you follow my advice, it won't be long before you see the wisdom of Buyers. By then, it will all make more sense to you—and you'll know how to sustain your love for a lifetime.

PART 4

"To Be Your Husband (or Wife)"

One Man, One Woman

13

Same-Sex Marriage a Threat?

Is There Anything Wrong with Gay and Lesbian Relationships?

Over the past thirty-five years, I've watched as our government has done just about everything imaginable to lose the meaning of traditional marriage. We've allowed the enactment of laws that suggest traditional marriage has become outdated—that a permanent and sexually exclusive relationship of extraordinary care is no longer relevant. And all this has occurred with very little resistance despite devastating consequences to our families and to society in general. In each case these laws were passed with hardly a murmur of opposition.

That's why I was shocked to witness the energy behind grassroots efforts to resist same-sex marriage. Why now? I must say that I honestly didn't understand how this issue could create such a firestorm of protest when so little opposition had arisen against earlier changes in laws regarding marriage. But whatever the reason, I was energized by the realization that the controversy had awakened a sleeping giant. And legislators were listening.

In response to the public outcry, legislators at first simply enacted laws against same-sex marriage, hoping that would be enough to satisfy their constituents. But when judges challenged those laws as being unconstitutional, it became apparent that nothing short of a constitutional amendment against same-sex marriage would suffice. So states throughout America are now in the process of changing their constitutions. They want to define marriage in their state constitutions as a relationship between one man and one woman—just so judges will not tamper with it.

From my perspective, traditional marriage was already doomed by the cultural bias against extraordinary care in marriage and by the passage of laws supporting infidelity and divorce. So what difference would it make if gays and lesbians "married," when marriage had already lost its traditional meaning? Based on the legal and cultural trends we've considered so far in this book, I had already predicted that traditional marriage would be reduced to a cultural footnote within the next few decades.

Consider the numbers. My best estimate of the percentage of marriages that suffer from infidelity is 60 percent. That's over half of all marriages. And the percentage of marriages that end in divorce is about 45 percent—almost half. In contrast, where same-sex marriage or civil unions are encouraged, they account for just 0.5 percent of all marriages. That means only five couples out of a thousand actually choose that path—99.5 percent choose heterosexual marriage.[1] How much influence could that half of one percent have on the rest of us?

So when I first became aware of the same-sex marriage issue, I didn't view it as a significant risk for traditional families. There were too few of them to have much impact. On the other hand, laws favoring infidelity and divorce have had, and continue to have, a devastating effect on marriage. It seemed to me that all of that energy going into avoiding same-sex marriage was being directed at the wrong issue. Traditional marriage was already on the rocks—and not because of the same-sex marriage issue.

Nonetheless, the more I studied the arguments both for and against same-sex marriage, the more convinced I became that the fourth element of marriage—that it is between a man and a woman—does need to be supported. Let me explain why I'm now on board.

Do Same-Sex Relationships Really Work?

Traditional marriage creates the most fulfilling relationship that is possible in life. When all four of its essential elements are in place, a husband and wife—and their children—are very happy. But when even one of those elements is lacking, trouble is on the horizon.

It's easy to see how the lack of extraordinary care, sexual exclusivity, or permanence would wreck a relationship. But is it all that important for the couple to be of opposite sexes?

Admittedly, there's not much published research on this topic. As with surveys that ask people about incidences of infidelity, it's difficult to obtain accurate data regarding fulfillment in same-sex relationships. In public surveys, most people will either deny ever having had an affair or, when they do admit it, will tend to downplay its disastrous consequences. Likewise, in surveys, same-sex couples who are fighting for the right to marry are likely to downplay frustration or dissatisfaction with their relationships.

But I've observed hundreds of same-sex couples in my own professional experience, and they have always

Can Gays and Lesbians Become Heterosexual?

I've heard most of the arguments used by gays and lesbians against the possibility of changing their sexual orientation. But I know from my counseling experience that it is possible. I've seen many who were same-sex oriented learn to become opposite-sex oriented. It's possible for these individuals to be just as attracted to and just as much in love with someone of the opposite sex.

The reverse is also true. Those who are attracted to the opposite sex can become attracted to the same sex. In fact, most of us can become sexually attracted to almost anything or anyone under certain conditions. Eliminate attractive opposite-sex alternatives, and people find that they can respond sexually to whatever happens to be available.

That's why I'm so concerned about educational programs in schools that teach children that we are born to be either same-sex oriented or opposite-sex oriented. In those early years when children are very impressionable, they may be influenced to believe they are gay or lesbian simply because they experience some same-sex interest.

Quite frankly, most children

stood out to me as being characteristically frustrated and depressed—many to the point of suicide. Same-sex relationships tend to be very brief and, especially for men, very unhealthy and violent. Granted, I've seen my share of unhealthy opposite-sex relationships as well. Yet on average, the same-sex relationships I've witnessed have been far more fragile.

For these and a host of other clinical reasons, I've discouraged my clients from maintaining their same-sex relationships. Instead I encourage them to either pull away from romantic relationships entirely for a time or to turn their attention to opposite-sex relationships. And, contrary to public perceptions, I've seen many clients successfully reorient themselves to opposite-sex relationships. Scores of my previously gay and lesbian clients are now at one time or another will find themselves sexually attracted to members of their own sex. If, as a result, they begin to focus their sexual attention on those of the same sex and create skills and neural pathways that make same-sex relationships far more satisfying than opposite-sex relationships, it's easy for them to think they were born to be gay. It becomes self-fulfilling prophecy. On the other hand, if they recognize such same-sex attraction as a natural response to certain circumstances but remain open to opposite-sex attractions that will also develop, they'll likely go on to pursue opposite-sex relationships that ultimately *will*

provide the stability and fulfillment they're looking for.

Sexual orientation is not determined by birth but rather by choice. The truth is that we are all capable of expressing our sexuality in ways that we haven't even considered yet.

People can become sexually oriented to just about anyone or anything. And they *can* change that orientation if there is good reason to do so. In the case of gays and lesbians, a change to opposite-sex orientation can help them achieve more fulfilling relationships for themselves. And it provides the best opportunity to raise happy and successful children as well.

happily married with children—all because they embraced a traditional definition of marriage that is marked by extraordinary care for life.

I have absolutely no doubt that same-sex relationships can be very romantic. And they can be characterized by the extraordinary care I've suggested. But even in the best of these relationships, when a couple has been honest with me, they have both admitted that they would have preferred feeling the same way toward someone of the opposite sex. The truth is, on average, opposite-sex relationships tend to be more stable and fulfilling. And that, in itself, is a good reason to promote traditional marriage rather than same-sex marriage. But there's also another, even more important reason: the welfare of our children.

A Biological Father and Mother Make the Best Parents

When parents share genetic traits with their children, it gives them an instinctive advantage for understanding what those children need. Shared genetic traits also tend to help children understand why their parents react the way they do. That emotional similarity helps parents and children form a bond that is much more difficult to form in alternative families. And that bond leads to trust that makes training much easier to implement.

Since gay and lesbian relationships do not lead to the creation of offspring that share genetic traits of *both* partners, they suffer a distinct disadvantage when it comes to raising children. At best, just one of the parents has that biological connection to the child. And as a result, they lack the same emotional empathy that biological parents tend to have.

Also, because gay or lesbian couples do not offer both a male and female parental role model for their children early in life, such children are at a distinct disadvantage later in life. In most families biological fathers and mothers tend to play very different roles in the training of children that help balance love and care (a mother's influence) with responsibility and discipline (a father's influence). Granted, I acknowledge a significant overlap in these traits—women are also responsible and disciplined, and men do demonstrate love and care. But in most families, care is more emphasized by mothers and responsibility is more emphasized by fathers.

A father gives his children insight into the way men tend to view the world, and a mother gives them a woman's perspective. As long as both parents respect each other's way of thinking, a child grows up with understanding of the value of both men and women. Diversity training begins in the traditional family, where children come

214

to appreciate the differences between their mother and father.

Same-sex couples offer children little hope of understanding and appreciating the differences between men and women because they cannot provide daily exposure to both a father *and* a mother. Instead, they tend to reinforce a false belief that men and women are not made for each other because they cannot demonstrate to children the exquisite way that a man and woman can blend together.

In addition to concerns about male and female parental influences, there is also another reason to be concerned about the ability of gay and lesbian couples to raise children most successfully: their relationships are notoriously unstable. As we've already discussed, problems they have trying to make their relationship fulfilling often cause them to jump from one relationship to another—in constant search of that perfect match. As a result, their relationships don't usually last very long. Only a very small percentage stay together long enough to raise a child to adulthood.

As I already mentioned, it's difficult to get accurate information about the stability of same-sex relationships from surveys. But the countries that have enacted laws granting same-sex marriage and civil unions have provided our first truly objective measures of the stability of same-sex marriages. For the first time, we have their divorce rates.

We are all aware how fragile opposite-sex marriages have been recently—divorce rates are incredibly high. In fact, one of the arguments used in support of same-sex marriage is that they can't be any worse than opposite-sex marriage. But the first solid evidence we have on that subject from Sweden is that same-sex marriages are worse—much worse.

215

In the Swedish study, the divorce rate of same-sex couples was compared with the divorce rate of opposite-sex couples over a similar period of time. It was found that same-sex male couples were 50 percent more likely to divorce, and same-sex female couples were 167 percent more likely to divorce than their opposite-sex counterparts. In other words, divorce statistics among same-sex couples reflected what I already knew—they are unstable whether or not they marry.[2]

And these results are particularly impressive when you consider that same-sex couples in the most stable relationships would be the first to take advantage of the opportunity to marry. The early results from Sweden should give same-sex couples a temporary advantage over their opposite-sex counterparts when divorce rates are compared. But this study indicates that the first group of same-sex couples to have married in Sweden are actually more likely to divorce than opposite-sex couples in the same culture. And I expect future studies to show the divorce rates of same-sex couples to be even higher.

If same-sex relationships are much less stable than opposite-sex relationships (as shown in the Swedish study), it should be obvious that they're not the ideal place for children to be raised. Children need safety and stability, and same-sex relationships tend to provide exactly the opposite—danger and instability.

In chapter 10, I presented other reasons why children need a biological father and mother who stay together, so I won't repeat them here. But I will repeat the conclusion of thousands of studies: the best way to raise happy and successful children is for them to be with their biological father and mother who are united in marriage and who love their children and each other. In other words, a same-sex couple simply cannot give children the advantages that biological parents are able to provide.

Why Experiment with the Lives of Children?

Many call same-sex marriage a social evolution. I'm in favor of new ways of doing things if they work. But I think same-sex marriage is more accurately characterized as a social experiment, and early results of this experiment are not at all encouraging. In fact, they are downright frightening, especially from the perspective of children.

Why experiment with the lives of our children? Even if only one-half of one percent of couples will exercise the option of same-sex marriage, it's still an unsafe and unstable environment for both them and the children they could raise.

Children will believe almost anything we tell them when they're young. So why give children the impression that same-sex relationships offer the same advantages as opposite-sex relationships when it's not true? And why would we want to mislead children into thinking that same-sex relationships are safe and secure when it's so clear that they're not? They are more violent, more unhealthy, and more unstable than their heterosexual counterparts.

Men and women are made for each other physically, emotionally, and spiritually. I am a witness to how successful and permanent a relationship between a

Rational Fear, Not Phobia

People who have discovered the truth about same-sex relationships and warn people to avoid them are called "homophobic." I admit that I'm afraid of same-sex relationships, but it's not because I'm "phobic." A phobia is an irrational fear of something that is harmless. But there is ample reason to fear same-sex relationships because of the damage they can do.

Parents who see a child drift into a same-sex relationship are terrified when it happens, and they continue to fear for their child's safety and happiness as long as the same-sex relationship continues. Why? It's because they see firsthand what it's doing to their child.

217

man and woman can be when they give each other extraordinary care.

Traditional marriages have suffered a body blow lately because our culture has failed to teach us the meaning of extraordinary care in marriage. And the same cultural changes that led to uncaring marriages also helped create the legal changes that made infidelity and divorce more common. Today, the success of marriage is at an all-time low when it comes to achieving its potential. But in spite of its failure, heterosexual marriage is still doing far better than its same-sex counterpart.

If men and women would give each other the extraordinary care they promise at the time of marriage, our society would not be so disillusioned with marriage, and as a result we wouldn't even be considering same-sex marriage these days. And we wouldn't be seeing much infidelity or divorce either. If our marriages were to be characterized by extraordinary care, the other three elements of marriage would be easy for everyone to understand and accept.

But since we've come so far in destroying three of the essential elements of traditional marriage, I'm delighted that the risk of losing the fourth element has finally drawn the public's attention to traditional marriage. Perhaps this effort to stop further erosion in marriage will eventually help restore the other elements that have been missing. If that happens, we will have helped create the quality of marriage that will make our children happier, healthier, and more successful than we could have ever imagined.

14

Is a Constitutional Amendment Really Necessary?

The Defense of Marriage Act

At the beginning of this book, I described the events surrounding a hastily prepared testimony that I gave before the Minnesota Senate Judiciary Committee. With that testimony I was asked to defend a bill that would give Minnesota residents the right to vote for or against a state constitutional amendment to limit legal marriage to one man and one woman. The amendment was named the Defense of Marriage Act (also known as DOMA) because those who proposed it believed that without it, the meaning of marriage would be eroded. Early polls indicated that voters would approve the amendment by a wide margin—70 percent or more. The bill itself, authored by Senator Michelle Bachmann, reads as follows:

> A bill for an act proposing an amendment to the Minnesota Constitution by adding a section to article XIII;

recognizing as marriage only a union between one man and one woman. BE IT ENACTED BY THE LEGISLATURE OF THE STATE OF MINNESOTA:
Sec. 1. [CONSTITUTIONAL AMENDMENT PROPOSED.] An amendment to the Minnesota Constitution is proposed to the people. If the amendment is adopted, a section shall be added to article XIII, to read: Sec. 13. Only the union of one man and one woman shall be valid or recognized as a marriage in Minnesota. Any other relationship shall not be recognized as a marriage or its legal equivalent.
Sec. 2. [QUESTION.] The proposed amendment shall be submitted to the people at the 2004 general election. The question submitted shall be: "Shall the Minnesota Constitution be amended to provide that only the union of one man and one woman will be recognized as a marriage in Minnesota? Yes . . . No . . ."

Short and sweet, right? "Shall the Minnesota Constitution be amended to provide that only the union of one man and one woman will be recognized as a marriage in Minnesota?" Yes or no. The wording was similar to many other constitutional amendments that were being proposed in state legislatures throughout America in the spring of 2004. And it eventually ended up on the ballots of eighteen states—Minnesota wasn't one of them.

The Minnesota Senate adjourned without having addressed a host of other important bills, simply because opponents of the Defense of Marriage Act didn't want this issue to be brought to the floor for debate. They realized that if it were debated, it would be passed. And if the proposed amendment were on the ballot in the fall, the people would vote to have the state constitution amended to define marriage as the union of one man and one woman.

That strategy—to keep issues affecting marriage away from the people—is pretty much the way that all attacks

220

on traditional marriage have survived. Even today, with families in shambles throughout America, people still basically support traditional marriage as the ideal. And that support was even greater when the first attacks began.

Quite frankly, if each of the attacks against permanence and sexual exclusivity in marriage had been made public, they would not have succeeded. We would still have laws today that punish those who seduce a spouse and laws that try to keep marriages together whenever possible.

But the same-sex marriage issue came at a unique time in history. Thanks to the Internet and an explosion of talk-show radio programming, the public is more aware than ever before of laws enacted by legislators and judges. It's almost impossible for lawmakers to do anything in secret anymore. I'm certain that if the Internet had been available to California residents in 1969, the bill favoring no-fault divorce would not have been passed. And laws that took away a spouse's right to sue for damages due to infidelity would not have been enacted either.

While opponents in Minnesota succeeded in keeping the issue of same-sex marriage from the people in 2004, that was not the case in other states. The residents of eighteen states were able to vote on a constitutional amendment limiting marriage to one man and one woman: Alaska, Arkansas, Georgia, Hawaii, Kansas, Kentucky, Louisiana, Michigan, Mississippi, Missouri, Montana, Nebraska, Nevada, North Dakota, Ohio, Oklahoma, Oregon, and Utah. In each of those states the amendment passed overwhelmingly.

So far, whenever the issue of same-sex marriage has been raised, the people have overwhelmingly supported traditional marriage. And that would have been the case if each aspect of traditional marriage had been presented to the public separately. Should it be illegal to have an affair with a married man or woman? Should married

Democracy and the Policy of Joint Agreement—the Problem with "Knowing Better"

Whenever our elected government representatives decide that the will of the people should be ignored, we're all in trouble. But when it comes to decisions regarding marriage, it's more than trouble—it's a disaster!

By failing to let the people of Minnesota decide the meaning of traditional marriage and giving themselves that right instead, these representatives are telling their constituents that they know better. They are saying that it's too complicated for the average mind to grasp. It's an issue far better understood and decided by professionals.

When I faced the Senate Judiciary Committee in Minnesota, I was facing legislators who felt that the people of Minnesota could not make a wise decision regarding this issue. They felt that same-sex marriage was a right that had to be granted to those who wanted it. They believed that to deny marriage to those with a same-sex orientation would be the same as sending black people to the back of the bus. Many argued that the right of gays and lesbians to marry was as important as any civil rights issue of the past one hundred years. If the people of Minnesota were to be given the right to decide the same-sex marriage issue, the legislators believed a mistake would be made. They had no confidence in the wisdom of the people.

It's really the same problem facing many marriages these

men or women have the right to sue someone for damages if their spouse was seduced? Should a spouse wanting a divorce show cause before it can be granted? Should the distribution of property and child custody in divorce be partly determined by proven fault?

While infidelity, fault, property distribution, and child custody are all difficult issues, the people want our courts to take them seriously. We don't want the courts to brush them away with laws that are designed to lower their caseload.

days. Husbands and wives often believe that their own opinions are so far superior to those of their spouse that unilateral decisions are necessary. Their failure to respect and take each other's opinions and interests into account when they make decisions contributes greatly to the failure of marriage. Such disregard for each other's opinions is not only thoughtless, but it prevents the wisest decisions from being made.

As I've repeated throughout this book, one of the cardinal rules for marriage is the Policy of Joint Agreement: *Never do anything without an enthusiastic agreement between you and your spouse.* It's a rule that turns a marital dictatorship into a marital democracy. It enables each spouse to defend his or her interests, preventing the other spouse from running roughshod over them. Those who favor this rule favor a marriage that's based on thoughtfulness and respect. Those who oppose it feel that the spouse who knows better—usually the husband—should make the decisions.

When spouses follow the Policy of Joint Agreement, the final result is in the interest of both spouses. They take far more into account than either spouse would have considered in making a final decision alone. The Policy of Joint Agreement promotes thoughtfulness and wisdom, and it helps build a mutually enjoyable lifestyle for both spouses.

The same thing can be said for a democracy. A true democracy recognizes that the will of the people is more thoughtful and wiser than decisions by a dictator. Democracy helps build a strong society better than anything that lawyers behind closed doors could ever create.

For those of us who support traditional marriage, the amendment of state constitutions is a step in the right direction. But is it enough?

A National Debate

Even if every state in America were to amend their constitutions to define marriage as the union of a man and a woman, there still remains a way that they could be overturned: an act of the United States Supreme Court. The Supreme Court could declare every one of those amendments to be in violation of the federal Constitution. That's why there has been an increasing effort to close that option by amending the U.S. Constitution to include the definition of traditional marriage. That, however, is not an easy task.

In Minnesota, the state constitution can be amended by a vote of its residents. If the legislature had passed the Defense of Marriage Act, granting the residents the right to vote on the definition of marriage, and a majority of the residents had then approved the DOMA at the November 2004 election, the state constitution would have been amended. Simple as that.

But it's much more difficult to amend the federal Constitution. First, two-thirds of each branch of the legislature must approve an amendment. Then the majority of the residents of at least thirty-eight of the fifty states must approve it within a five-year period. Only after all of that does it become part of our Constitution.

The latest wording of the Marriage Protection Amendment being considered in the U.S. Senate is: "Marriage in the United States shall consist only of the union of a man and a woman. Neither this Constitution, nor the constitution of any State, shall be construed to require that marriage or the legal incidents thereof be conferred upon any union other than the union of a man and a woman" (S.J. Res. 40).

Amendments to the federal Constitution were granted because its originators knew that clarification of its intent would be needed in the future. And marriage certainly qualifies as an issue needing clarification. So it's likely that an effort will be made in the next few years to add an amendment to the federal Constitution defining marriage as the union of a man and a woman.

If the issue were left up to the people to decide, I'm confident that more than three-quarters of the states would approve it. In fact, I'd be very surprised if anything less than all fifty states give it their support.

DOMA and Same-Sex Couples

Many opponents to the Defense of Marriage Amendment believe that such legal action to prevent same-sex marriage is discriminatory and destructive to same-sex couples. But when a government encourages gay and lesbian individuals to marry, it really isn't doing them any favors. These relationships are notoriously dangerous and fragile, and to encourage marriage in those cases serves only to prolong that danger and fragility.

It wasn't too many years ago that the psychiatric profession characterized homosexuality as a mental illness, and there was plenty of evidence to support that characterization. Mental health specialists noticed the same tendency toward violence and depression that I noticed when treating those with a same-sex orientation. And when these patients were shown how to change their sexual orientation, their whole outlook on life improved, ending their misery.

Today, when individuals with a same-sex orientation visit a therapist, they are told that their depression is caused by the failure of society to accept them as they are. Few point out that their depression may be caused by the venereal disease they've contracted in the past year, or the failure of three relationships in the past month, or their feeling of hopelessness whenever they realize that they will never be part of a traditional family.

Instead, they are told to be proud of the way they are—to celebrate the sexual orientation that's making their lives miserable. Just as the word *pride* is designed to sweep away any nagging questions about the value of same-sex relationships, the word *gay* gives the false impression that those in that lifestyle are always happy and never depressed.

By helping gays and lesbians change their sexual orientation and control their sexual impulses, I helped scores of people overcome sexually contracted diseases, create stable relationships, and eventually become part of a traditional family. There are still many, like myself, who are trained to achieve that objective, but we're no longer in the mainstream of mental health. In fact, our culture has now come to a point where those who provide such therapy are judged by many to be immoral.

I know of many therapists and clergymen who have simply given up on those with a same-sex orientation. They've been so battered and bruised by unrelenting attacks on themselves and their families that they have washed their hands of them all. And many European governments have done the same thing. Why not let them marry? It's their lives that are at risk—let them suffer the consequences.

I don't believe that same-sex marriages will destroy traditional marriages. There are simply too few of them to make much of a difference. But I'm sure that same-sex relationships tend to destroy most of those who have them. And it's a very bad idea to try to use marriage as a way to prolong those unhealthy relationships. As I've already mentioned, emerging data on same-sex marriage in Europe supports what we already knew: marriage will not make same-sex relationships any safer or more secure. Also, it distorts the real meaning of marriage.

Marriage is instituted primarily to form a safe and secure environment for the offspring of a man and a woman. It is a social convention that encourages parents to give their children a great start in life. But it's a terrible misuse of a valuable tradition to use it as an attempted cure for the problems of same-sex relationships.

So rather than discriminating against same-sex couples, an amendment to protect the definition of marriage as being between a man and a woman actually helps those couples. It does this by preventing them from striving to experience the positive results of traditional marriage without one of the major conditions that make those marriages successful—the condition that marriage is between a man and a woman.

A Slippery Slope

It makes sense for traditional marriage to be limited to one man and one woman. But it's important to note that if our legislatures and courts are successful in overturning that tradition, same-sex couples would not be the only ones to be affected. It would affect a host of other alternative living arrangements as well. Most notably, polygamy—the marriage of an individual to more than one man or woman.

Unlike same-sex marriage, which has not been tolerated in any civilization or religion in world history, polygamous marriage has not only been tolerated, but it was encouraged by most governments and religions prior to the birth of Christ. Even today, there are many countries that allow polygamy.

If marriage is no longer to be defined as a relationship between one man and one woman, why not let it be between several men and several women?

Over the past two thousand years, largely influenced by Christianity, Western civilization has demonstrated the value of limiting marriage to one man and one woman. There are few today who would argue that polygamy is at all desirable. And there are people in prison for testing the law against it. But there is far less evidence for the danger and instability of polygamous marriages than there is for same-sex marriages. For example, in those cases biological parents raise their children. So when adults in these relationships agree to marry, why should the government stand in their way if the mold of traditional marriage has already been broken?

I don't know how you feel about polygamy, but I'm actually more opposed to it than I am to same-sex marriage. That's because once it is allowed, there will be far more polygamous marriages than there will be same-sex marriages. In fact, it may eventually become the rule rather than the exception, just as it has been in past civilizations.

Same-sex relationships will never be the rule in any culture because they simply don't work as well as opposite-sex relationships do. We were not created to have them. In spite of laws, misguided educational programs, and entertainment that portray these relationships as being desirable, they actually leave most people perpetually miserable. But polygamy has worked in the past, and if it's allowed to exist in the present, I fear that it may eventually become the norm.

Incidentally, another type of marital relationship with historical precedent is that between children and adults. Why shouldn't marriage be legal for a thirty-five-year-old man and a twelve-year-old girl? It has happened throughout history and still exists in many of our contemporary cultures. If we do not limit marriage to a man and woman, why limit it at all? Why not allow for the inclusion of children as well?

When marriage is anything other than the union of one man and one woman, we create a social nightmare. That's because man and woman are made for each other, and they are made to create the very best environment for their children. Children flourish the most in the context of the marriage of their father and their mother. So why experiment with the lives of our children when we already know what works?

When I was first introduced to the idea of a constitutional amendment to protect marriage, I thought it was a joke, or at least a very bad idea. But now that I clearly see the threat of marriage losing its traditional meaning, I'm a firm supporter of the amendment. I hope that the Minnesota Constitution eventually contains an amendment that defines marriage as the union of one man and one woman. And I also hope that we will amend our federal Constitution in the same way.

15

Restoring the Meaning of Traditional Marriage

How the Same-Sex Marriage Issue Has Helped Raise Public Awareness

In spite of the importance of traditional marriage to children, to men and women, and to our entire country, it hasn't been given much attention—until recently. And that lack of attention has given marriage-unfriendly politicians free rein to create marriage-unfriendly laws. The erosion of traditional marriage over the past seventy years, both legally and culturally, has taken place because the public has been asleep at the switch. The vast majority of Americans have been either unaware of or disinterested in what was going on behind closed doors. Radio, television, and newspapers barely gave the subject a glancing notice.

When I began my profession as a marriage counselor, many of my colleagues already felt that marriage had become obsolete. They believed it was a trap for women and that it prevented just about everyone from achieving their full potential. I was told that children would do far better if raised by a single parent than by parents who were in conflict with each other. And I was challenged by the questions: What marriage doesn't eventually go sour? What couple doesn't eventually grow apart?

Many of the marriage counselors I knew didn't try to save marriages. Instead, they told struggling couples that their marriage was not worth saving and that their children would be better off if they were divorced.

Today, studies have proven that children thrive when their parents stay married, even when they're in conflict, and they struggle when they are born out of wedlock or when their parents divorce. Just about everyone now realizes that marriage is the ideal environment for raising children. In fact, both state and federal governments are beginning to encourage couples to stay together rather than encouraging them to divorce. Marriage leads to prosperity and taxpaying citizens, while divorce and single parenting lead to poverty and a drain on our economy.

One of the first steps taken by the federal government to encourage marriage was the federal welfare reform legislation enacted in 1996. After thirty years of effectually paying unwed mothers to bear children, both Republicans and Democrats could see that the welfare system was hurting the very people it was intended to help. The substantial incentives given to women who avoided marriage and weren't earning a living were trapping women in poverty and making them victims of abuse. Their children dropped out of high school, convinced that education and employment were for fools. And our prisons grew to overflowing with those who were the recipients of marriage-destroying government policy.

So a logical step was taken by some of the very politicians who had created the problem—they took away financial incentives to bear children out of wedlock. The time that a woman could receive most welfare benefits was limited to five years, and job training was required while benefits were being received to create self-sufficiency. As a result, welfare roles were greatly reduced, and the incentive to marry was greatly increased. We are already seeing some of the benefits of this change with increased school attendance and reduction in crime for children raised in poverty.

The stated goal of welfare reform was to help increase the number of two-parent families and to reduce out-of-wedlock childbearing. By simply changing the law, we've started to solve a problem that the law helped create.

I do not think that our state and federal governments must make a major financial investment in the restoration of marriages. I'm convinced that marriage will recover if they simply eliminate the marriage-unfriendly laws that have been enacted over the past seventy years. Now that the issue of same-sex marriage has drawn the public's attention, perhaps the time is also right for laws that encourage infidelity and divorce to be rescinded.

In my effort to bring these marriage-unfriendly laws to the attention of legislators, I've noticed that those who are strongly in favor of limiting marriage to the union of a man and a woman have been very receptive to my suggestion that all marriage-unfriendly laws be rescinded. Without hesitation, they want to help create new marriage-friendly laws.

I believe that most voters feel the same way. Since the last election, the people have sent their representatives a convincing message: they are opposed to same-sex marriage. And if given a chance to make their opinions known about the two other aspects of marriage, infidelity and divorce, I am convinced that they will also support legislation that discourages all marriage-crippling laws.

We can take a lesson from the way in which the same-sex marriage issue is being decided. It's not from the top down—it's from the bottom up. The astonishing grassroots attention given to the issue of same-sex marriage has made it possible for the wisdom of the people to correct the mistakes of their representatives.

Restoring Sexual Exclusivity to Marriage

Our laws define our values. When we enact laws against infidelity, we send the message that an affair is wrong. Even if damages cannot be proven in a court of law, it's wrong. And when damages can be proven, those responsible should be held liable for those damages.

The way it stands today in most states, our laws protect people who have affairs. In spite of damages that can be proven in court, it's not possible to claim them. In other words, our current laws send the following message to those who would attack marriage through seduction: Have as many affairs as you wish. Our laws will protect you.

In contrast, current law does *not* protect the betrayed spouse who tries to ward off an interloper. Someone can invade a marriage with impunity, yet the victim is sent to prison if he or she attacks the invader in any way.

Websites are springing up all over the Internet that offer to help people initiate affairs. And books are written to explain how to best seduce spouses. It's been my experience over the years that the incidence of infidelity has grown steadily, largely because it's legal. After all, our laws tell us what's right and what's wrong. And since there are no laws against infidelity, people who are tempted think it must not be wrong.

234

In spite of laws that make your marriage vulnerable to infidelity, you can protect your marriage by taking the extraordinary precautions that I took when I first married Joyce (see chapter 9). But if you would like to protect other marriages, join a grassroots effort to reinstate laws against infidelity.

Let your legislative representatives know that you would like to see laws against infidelity enacted. And while you're at it, discuss the position held by your representative on the subject of same-sex marriage. Talk to him or her about the pros and cons of instituting legal protection for your family. Is your representative representing you? Are the laws that your representative helps to enact supporting your interests and values?

Restoring Permanence to Marriage

No-fault divorce law also sends a message. It says that the covenant of marriage is so trivial that those entering that contract do not need a justifiable reason to break it. If one person feels that the marriage is not working out, that person can end it without finding fault with his or her spouse.

This law was originally proposed as a way to make divorce less adversarial. It was argued by many who proposed the law that couples would have a greater opportunity to reconcile if they could approach divorce in a friendly, less confrontational way. And while a couple was going through divorce, a new family court system would shepherd them back to marital health.

But that didn't happen. Since fault is still relevant in child custody and property settlement issues, divorces remain ugly. And the family court system that was originally proposed was either totally rejected or it was of little help to couples. No-fault divorce law has not made reconciliation easier—it has made divorce easier.

It's as if legislators enacted a law that allowed you to break a loan contract without a reason to do so. They would have argued that no-fault loan law would make it easier for people to pay off their loans. Even if you have adequate income to make the payments and you don't qualify for bankruptcy, you could simply walk away from a loan. After obtaining the loan from the bank and buying a new boat, you decide that it's not in your best interest to make the payments. You'd rather spend that money on something else. If such no-fault loan laws were enacted, what effect would that law have on the lending industry? Banks would be going out of business.

The same thing is happening in marriage. Marriages are going out of business. Every year the rate of new marriage in America decreases and the average age of couples marrying increases. Couples are waiting longer to marry, wanting to get to know each other better. They know how devastating divorce is and how the law offers them absolutely no protection from a spouse's momentary change of attitude. As a result, more couples are living together before marriage, in spite of the fact that it's the most dangerous environment for women and children (see chapter 10). They'd rather face the danger of violence than the danger that divorce creates.

We need laws that support the covenant of marriage. All legal contracts can be broken only if there is cause. Why should the contract of marriage be any different than the rest? If one spouse has an affair, is abusive, abandons the other spouse, or does anything that qualifies for cause, our laws should permit divorce. And there should be a penalty for violating a marriage contract just as there is for violating any other contract. In the case of marriage, the penalty should be reflected in financial support and in the division of property. In other words, just like in all other contracts, cause for divorce would require just compensation to the blameless spouse.

Some argue that both spouses are to blame in a divorce. But my thirty-five years of experience as a marriage counselor does not bear out that common belief. I know of many, if not most, marriages that suffer because only one spouse has been irresponsible. One spouse, not both, has an affair. One, not both, is physically violent. One, not both, abandons the family. Besides, if it can be shown in a court of law that both spouses are equally to blame, so be it. But why assume that's the case before they've even gone to trial?

When I counsel a couple, I know early on what changes must be made to make the marriage successful. And I know who must make the changes. By establishing fault in a divorce action, the court is simply telling each spouse how the marriage agreement has been broken. The assignment of fault does not make divorce more adversarial—its decision points out how reconciliation might be possible.

The way it is right now, the court assumes that no one is to blame for the divorce—no fault. In other words, it draws the false and outrageous conclusion that there is no known way to restore the marriage. It's called "irreconcilable differences." But I know that almost every marriage is reconcilable. That's why I guarantee marital recovery for any couple willing to follow my advice. The court is perpetrating a lie when it tells a divorcing couple that no one is to blame for their divorce and that there is no way to heal their marriage.

A couple I recently counseled was in the process of divorcing. The offense? The husband's failure to clean up the yard—it had turned into a junkyard. The solution seemed rather simple, but in the state where they live, the court isn't interested in causes or solutions. The wife would have been granted a divorce for "irreconcilable differences." But she told me that she would drop the divorce if the yard were cleaned up. Until I spoke with her, the husband was completely unaware that there was anything he could do to save his marriage. He cleaned up the yard, and she dropped the divorce action.

Of course most marriages are not as easy to save. But they all share the same general solution. If a husband and wife make changes to provide extraordinary care to each other, marriages can be saved. Spouses must learn to meet each other's important emotional needs, avoid hurting each other, and create a lifestyle that's mutually enjoyable. Failure in any of those areas is cause for divorce because it's a violation of the marriage agreement. And reconciliation simply means going back to the original agreement and keeping those promises. We need laws that address violations of the marriage agreement so that the terms of reconciliation can be clearly stated.

But even though there are no laws to protect your marriage covenant, you can protect it yourself by guaranteeing each other the extraordinary care you promised at the time of your wedding. That care will not only keep you together for life, but it will also keep you in love for life.

You can also help protect the marriages of others by encouraging your state and federal representatives to enact laws that require cause for divorce. If you're willing to talk to your legislative representatives about rescinding laws that protect infidelity, as I suggested earlier in this chapter, while you're there, also express your concern that existing no-fault divorce law threatens all of the families that he or she represents. Explain to your representative how a change in the law that reinstates cause for divorce will send a message that the government wants to encourage the fulfillment of the marriage agreement.

Restoring Extraordinary Care to Traditional Marriage

The meaning of traditional marriage doesn't begin with sexual exclusivity, permanence, or the union of a man and a woman. It begins with extraordinary care. That's because without it, marriage makes no sense. And with it, infidelity, divorce, and same-sex marriage make no sense.

It's my opinion that the most significant purpose for marriage is to raise the offspring of a husband and wife in the best environment possible—one that's safe and secure. Granted, there are many other reasons to marry even when no children will ever be involved. But quality parenting is so crucial to our society that it makes all of the other advantages of marriage pale in comparison.

Yet, without extraordinary care for each other, it's impossible for parents to raise their children successfully. As the most important examples their children will have in life, parents teach their children important values by the way they treat each other. If they are selfish and thoughtless toward each other, they teach their children to behave that way as adults—a formula for a lifetime of disappointment. But if they provide extraordinary care toward each other, they teach their children how to be successful in life by being thoughtful and caring toward others.

If a man and woman understand the meaning of extraordinary care at the time they say their vows, the other elements of marriage fall easily into place—sexual exclusivity and permanence become a very natural consequence.

Sexual exclusivity is absolutely essential in marriage for a host of reasons. But at the top of the list is the fact that an affair is the cruelest blow any spouse can inflict on the other. When compared with other examples of catastrophic loss, it's been consistently judged to be among the very worst. If at the time of marriage you had known that your spouse would be unfaithful, you would have called off the ceremony. No one wants to be married to an unfaithful spouse.

Yet what should you do if your spouse isn't willing to meet your sexual need? You've promised to "forsake all others," only to discover that your spouse isn't willing to meet your need for sex. Does marriage mean that you risk a life of celibacy?

Extraordinary care eliminates that risk. When a man and a woman promise to be faithful, they also promise to fulfill each other's sexual needs—and to meet all the other important emotional needs, including intimate conversation, affection, recreational companionship, honesty and openness, physical attractiveness, and admiration.

Permanence is also essential in marriage. It enables a couple to build the very best environment for their children and for each other. But the vow to remain married "until death do us part" makes sense only when extraordinary care is assumed. When you agreed to remain married "in joy and in sorrow, in sickness and in health, in plenty and in want," you weren't agreeing to occasional beatings by your spouse as part of the bargain. And you were not agreeing to abandonment, deceit, or any of the other Love Busters mentioned earlier. Instead, you were agreeing to stay married when sources of trouble outside your control temporarily take some of the joy out of your marriage. In other words, you'd stick it out together when the going got tough—as long as you were providing extraordinary care for each other. Adversity strikes almost every couple at some time during their lives. The vow of permanence makes it clear that when these outside forces tempt spouses to run for cover, they will run to each other instead of running away.

Adversity in life is usually short-lived. The conditions that make life miserable usually dissipate in less than

Changing Marriage-Unfriendly Laws in Your State

If you would like some help and direction in changing some of the marriage-unfriendly laws in your state, I encourage you to contact the Institute for Marriage and Public Policy (iMAPP). This nonprofit "think tank" provides innovative research, technical expertise, and ideas for ways that law and public policy can strengthen marriage as a social institution. Divorce law reform, adoption policy, same-sex marriage, and unmarried childbearing are among their fields of expertise. Maggie Gallagher, who wrote the foreword for this book, is president of iMAPP and has been an intellectual leader on marriage. She is also co-author of one of the best summaries of marriage research that is available, "The Case for Marriage: Why Married People Are Happier, Healthier, and Better-Off Financially." She can help you formulate the wording on new laws, explain effective procedure, and put you in contact with those in your state who have similar goals. Visit her website at www.marriagedebate.com and email Joshua Baker at joshua@imapp.org for more information.

two years. So if couples can hang together in the face of life's storms, they usually find that their care for each other is particularly meaningful during that time. Instead of tearing a couple apart, the problems of life can draw them together—if they maintain their extraordinary care for each other.

I hope that our exploration of traditional marriage has convinced you that it's something worth defending. It creates one of the most fulfilling relationships you can experience in life. And it is essential for effective parenting.

During the past seventy years, our laws and culture have turned against traditional marriage. And it has had a crippling effect on millions of Americans who have been deprived of the advantages of strong marriages and

241

healthy families. But in spite of these influences working against traditional marriage, you can have a happy and successful marriage. The principles we've discussed in this book will help you inoculate your marriage from cultural and legal pressures that try to destroy it.

I challenge you to provide extraordinary care in your own marriage. Talk to your state and federal representatives about the importance of defending traditional marriage. And talk to your friends and neighbors as well. By standing together we can not only preserve our own marriages but also turn the tide of cultural and legal opinion to promote traditional marriage for generations to come.

Notes

Chapter 1 What's the Fuss All About?

1. Cynthia Harper and Sara McLanahan, "Father Absence and Youth Incarceration" (paper presented at the annual meeting of the American Sociological Association, San Francisco, 1998). Also, Elaine Ciulla Kamarck and William A. Galston, *Putting Children First: A Progressive Family Policy for the 1990s* (Washington, D.C.: Progressive Policy Institute, September 1990).

2. Linda J. Waite and Maggie Gallagher, *The Case for Marriage: Why Married People Are Happier, Healthier, and Better Off Financially* (New York: Broadway Books, 2000).

Chapter 3 How to Make Each Other Happy

1. Willard F. Harley Jr., *His Needs, Her Needs: Building an Affair-Proof Marriage* (Grand Rapids: Revell, 2001); Willard F. Harley Jr., *Five Steps to Romantic Love* (Grand Rapids: Revell, 2002); and Georgia Kline-Graber, R.N., and Benjamin Graber, M.D., *Women's Orgasm: A Guide to Sexual Satisfaction* (New York: Warner Books, 1975).

Chapter 6 Our Culture and Care Don't Mix

1. Robert Stein, ed., *Why Young Mothers Feel Trapped: A Redbook Documentary* (New York: Trident Press, 1965).

2. Michael Gurian, "The Science of a Happy Marriage," *Reader's Digest*, August 2004, 151–55.

3. Locke Rush, *The True Marriage* (Philadelphia: ILM House, LLC, 2003).

4. Gurian, "The Science of a Happy Marriage," 155.

5. Names have been changed to protect the individuals' confidentiality.

Chapter 7   One of Life's Most Devastating Experiences

1. Tom W. Smith, *American Sexual Behavior: Trends, Socio-Demographic Differences, and Risk Behavior*, National Opinion Research Center (Chicago: University of Chicago, 2003).

2. William R. Corbett, "A Somewhat Modest Proposal to Prevent Adultery and Save Marriages: Two Old Torts Looking for a New Career," *Arizona State Law Journal* 33 (Winter 2001): 985–1055.

Chapter 8   The Law Is Wrong

1. Frederick L. Kane, "Heart Balm and Public Policy," *Fordham Law Review* 5 (1936): 63.

2. *1935 Indiana Acts*, chapter 208, section 1 (codified at Ind. Code. Ann. Section 2-508 [Burns 1946 replacement volume]).

3. Corbett, "A Somewhat Modest Proposal to Prevent Adultery and Save Marriages."

Chapter 9   How to Affair-Proof Your Marriage

1. This book is a 2001 edition of the book originally published by Revell in 1986.

2. Willard F. Harley Jr. and Jennifer Harley Chalmers, *Surviving an Affair* (Grand Rapids: Revell, 1998).

Chapter 10   When Is It Time to Call It Quits?

1. Nicholas Zill et al., "Long-Term Effects of Parental Divorce on Parent-Child Relationships, Adjustment, and Achievement and Young Adulthood," *Journal of Family Psychology* 7, no. 1 (1993): 91–103.

2. E. Mavis Hetherington and John Kelly, *For Better or For Worse: Divorce Reconsidered* (New York: W.W. Norton, 2002).

3. Paul R. Amato and Alan Booth, *A Generation at Risk: Growing Up in an Era of Family Upheaval* (Cambridge: Harvard University Press, 1997).

4. Pamela J. Smock et al., "The Effect of Marriage and Divorce on Women's Economic Well-Being," *American Sociological Review* 64 (1999): 794–812; Ross Finie, "Women, Men and the Economic Consequences of Divorce: Evidence from Canadian Longitudinal Data," *Canadian Review of Sociology and Anthropology* 30, no. 2 (1993): 205ff.; Teresa A. Mauldin, "Women Who Remain Above the Poverty Level in Divorce: Implications for Family Policy," *Family Relations* 39, no. 2 (1990): 141ff.

5. Donna K. Gunther and Madeline Zavodny, "Is the Male Marriage Premium Due to Selection? The Effect of Shotgun Weddings on the Return to Marriage," *Journal of Population Economics* 14 (2001): 313–28.

6. Waite and Gallagher, *The Case for Marriage*, 97–109.

7. Lingxin Hao, "Family Structure, Private Transfers, and the Economic Well-Being of Families with Children," *Social Forces* 75 (1996): 269–92.

8. Paul R. Amato, "Children of Divorce in the 1990s: An Update of the Amato and Keith (1991) Meta-Analysis," *Journal of Family Psychology* 15, no. 3 (2001): 355–70; William H. Jeynes, "The Effects of Several of the Most Common Family Structures on the Academic Achievement of Eighth Graders," 30, no. 1/2 (2000): 73–97; Catherine E. Ross and John Mirowsky, "Parental Divorce, Life-Course Disruption, and Adult Depression," *Journal of Marriage and the Family* 61, no. 4 (November 1999): 1034ff.; Sarah McLanahan and Gary Sandefur, *Growing Up With a Single Parent: What Hurts, What Helps* (Cambridge: Harvard University Press, 1994).

9. William H. Jeynes, "Effects of Remarriage Following Divorce on the Academic Achievement of Children," *Journal of Youth and Adolescence* 28, no. 3 (1999): 385–93; Nicholas Zill et al., "Long-Term Effects of Parental Divorce on Parent-Child Relationships."

10. Jane Mauldon, "The Effects of Marital Disruption on Children's Health," *Demography* 27 (1990): 431–46.

11. J. E. Schwartz et al., "Childhood Sociodemographic and Psychosocial Factors as Predictors of Mortality Across the Life-Span," *American Journal of Public Health* 85 (1995): 1237–45.

12. Joan S. Tucker et al., "Parental Divorce: Effects on Individual Behavior and Longevity," *Journal of Personality and Social Psychology* 73, no. 2 (1997): 381–91.

13. Paul R. Amato, "The Consequences of Divorce for Adults and Children," *Journal of Marriage and the Family* 62, no. 4 (2000): 1269ff.; Linda Waite and Mary Elizabeth Hughes, "At the Cusp of Old Age: Living Arrangements and Functional Status among Black, White and Hispanic Adults," *Journal of Gerontology: Social Sciences* 54b, no. 3 (1999): S136–44.

14. Yuanreng Hu and Noreen Goldman, "Mortality Differences by Marital Status: An International Comparison," *Demography* 27, no. 2 (1990): 233–50.

15. Amy Mehraban Pienta et al., "Health Consequences of Marriage for the Retirement Years," *Journal of Family Issues* 21, no. 5 (2000): 559–96.

16. E. Mavis Hetherington and John Kelly, *For Better or For Worse: Divorce Reconsidered* (New York: W.W. Norton, 2002); Paul R. Amato, "Children of Divorce in the 1990s"; Judith S. Wallerstein et al., *The Unexpected Legacy of Divorce: A 25 Year Landmark Study* (New York: Hyperion, 2000); Paul R. Amato, "The Consequences of Divorce for Adults and Children," *Journal of Marriage and the Family* 62, no. 4 (2000): 1269ff; Ronald L. Simons et al., "Explaining the Higher Incidence of Adjustment Problems among Children of Divorce Compared with Those in Two-Parent Families," *Journal of Marriage and the Family* 61, no. 4 (November 1999): 1020ff.; Judith Wallerstein and Sandra Blakeslee, *Second Chances: Men, Women and Children a Decade after Divorce* (New York: Ticknor and Fields, 1989).

17. Gregory R. Johnson et al., "Suicide among Adolescents and Young Adults: A Cross-National Comparison of 34 Countries," *Suicide and Life-Threatening Behavior* 30, no. 1 (2000): 74–82; David Lester, "Domestic Integration and Suicide in 21 Nations, 1950–1985," *International Journal of Comparative Sociology* 35, no. 1–2 (1994): 313–137.

18. David M. Cutler et al., "Explaining the Rise in Youth Suicide" (working paper 7713, National Bureau of Economic Research, Cambridge, MA, May 2000).

19. Ronald C. Kessler et al., "Prevalence of and Risk Factors for Lifetime Suicide Attempts in the National Comorbidity Survey," *Archives of General Psychiatry* 56 (1999): 617–26.

20. Sherryl H. Goodman et al., "Social and Emotional Competence in Children of Depressed Mothers," *Child Development* 64 (1993): 516–31.

21. Cynthia Harper and Sara McLanahan, "Father Absence and Youth Incarceration" (paper presented at the annual meeting of the American Sociological Association, San Francisco, August 1998).

22. Chris Coughlin and Samuel Vuchinich, "Family Experience in Preadolescence and the Development of Male Delinquency," *Journal of Marriage and the Family* 58, no. 2 (1996): 491ff.; R. J. Sampson and J. H. Laub, "Urban Poverty and the Family Context of Delinquency: A New Look at Structure and Process in a Classic Study," *Child Development* 65 (1994): 523–40; Robert J. Sampson, "Urban Black Violence: The Effect of Male Joblessness and Family Disruption," *American Journal of Sociology* 93 (1987): 348–82.

23. Ross L. Matsueda and Keren Heimer, "Race, Family Structure and Delinquency: A Test of Differential Association and Social Control Theories," *American Sociological Review* 52 (1987): 171–81.

24. Ronet Bachman, "Violence against Women," *National Crime Victimization Survey Report NCK-145325* (Washington, D.C.: U.S. Department of Justice, Office of Justice Programs, Bureau of Justice Statistics, January 1994): see tables 2 and 3.

25. John H. Laub et al., "Trajectories of Change in Criminal Offending: Good Marriages and the Desistance Process," *American Sociological Review* 63 (1998): 225–38.

26. Nicky Ali Jackson, "Observational Experiences of Intrapersonal Conflict and Teenage Victimization: A Comparative Study among Spouses and Cohabitors," *Journal of Family Violence* 11 (1996): 191–203.

27. Margo I. Wilson and Martin Daly, "Who Kills Whom in Spouse Killings? On the Exceptional Sex Ratio of Spousal Homicides in the United States," *Criminology* 30, no. 2 (1992): 189–215; J. E. Straus and M. A. Stets, "The Marriage License as Hitting License: A Comparison of Assaults in Dating, Cohabiting and Married Couples," *Journal of Family Violence* 4, no. 2 (1989): 161–80.

28. Martin Daly and Margo Wilson, "Child Abuse and Other Risks of Not Living with Both Partners," *Ethology and Sociobiology* 6 (1985): 197–210.

29. Leslie Margolin, "Child Abuse by Mothers' Boyfriends: Why the Overrepresentation?" *Child Abuse & Neglect* 16 (1992): 541–51.

Chapter 11   Is "No-Fault" at Fault?

1. *Laws of New York*, 1966, chapter 254.

2. *Arkansas Acts*, 1937, no. 167; *Arkansas Statutes*, annotated edition (Charlottesville: Michie, 1985), title 34-1202.

3. Oklahoma Statues Annotated (St. Paul: West Publishing, 1961), with 1985 supplement, title 12, par. 1271.

4. *Vernon's Texas Codes Annotated* (St. Paul: West Publishing, 1975), with 1986 supplement, title 3.01–08.

5. *Putting Asunder: A Divorce Law for Contemporary Society*, report of a group appointed by the Archbishop of Canterbury in January 1964 (London: S.P.C.K., 1966), 39.

6. Governor's Commission on the Family, "Final Report," December 15, 1966, typescript.

7. M. E. P. Seligman, "The Effectiveness of Psychotherapy: The *Consumer Reports* Study," *American Psychologist* 50 (1995): 965–74.

8. *Regular Session of the California Legislature* (1969), section 4506 (1) of chapter 1608s.

9. Henry H. Foster Jr., "Divorce Reform and the Uniform Act," *South Dakota Law Review* 18 (1973): 578.

10. Doris Jonas Freed, "Grounds for Divorce in the American Jurisdiction as of June 1, 1974," *Family Law Quarterly* 8 (1974): 401.

11. The fifteen states that completely eliminated cause for divorce were California (1969), Iowa (1970), Colorado (1971), Florida (1971), Michigan (1971), Oregon (1971), Kentucky (1972), Nebraska (1972), Arizona (1973), Missouri (1973), Washington (1973), Minnesota (1974), Delaware (1974), Montana (1975), and Wisconsin (1977).

12. Michael Reagan, *Twice Adopted* (Nashville: Broadman & Holman Publishers, 2004), 44.

13. "Fox Steps on an Industry's Toes," *The Middletown Journal* (Middletown, OH), July 30, 2003, electronically retrieved at http://www.stolenvows.com/fox.htm.

Chapter 13 Same-Sex Marriage a Threat?

1. Gunnar Andersson et al., "Divorce-Risk Patterns in Same-Sex 'Marriages' in Norway and Sweden" (paper presented at the annual meeting of the Population Association of America, April 3, 2004, available at http://paa2004.princeton.edu/download.asp?submissionId=40208).

2. Ibid.

Index

abandonment 240
abuse 97, 167, 197
addiction 88, 94–95, 133, 155, 156
admiration 35, 48, 166
adoption 241
adultery 119
    as grounds for divorce 177, 188
adversity 240
affairs 15–16, 234, 239–40
    addiction to 133
    denial of 152
    ending of 154–56
    freedom to have 123
    illegality of 221
    suffering from 113–14
affection 35, 36, 39–43, 46, 119, 146, 148, 150–51, 162, 166
AIDS 131
alienation of affection 115–16, 117–19, 126
alimony 185
American Bar Association 186, 187, 188
anarchy 82
Anarchy Strategy 79–80
Anglican (Episcopal) Church, on divorce 180
angry outbursts 39, 53, 58–61, 81, 83, 85, 97
annoying habits 53, 63–65
apology 157
Archbishop of Canterbury 180–81
attractive habits 65

bachelor parties 160
Bachmann, Michelle 219
balance 38
biological parents 214, 216
blackmail 123, 125, 126–27
blame, in divorce 237
blended lifestyle 102–3
brainstorming 85–87
breach of promise 123–25
Brown, Edmund 180
busy-ness, of married couples 95
buyers 197–205

California, divorce laws 179–85, 187
care 15
career 152
caring love 28–29
Catholic Church 187
Chalmers, Jennifer Harley 154
child custody 222
childcare 96
children 12–13, 16
    and divorce 17, 165–66, 168, 170–71, 173–74, 176, 189–90
    and infidelity 140–41
    marriage to adults 228
    of same-sex couples 213, 216
civil lawsuits 114–16, 137–38, 139
civil rights 9

codependency movement 94–95
cohabitation 167, 174
commitment 22
communication training 200–1
compatibility 63, 86, 102–3
consenting adults 131–34
constitutional amendment 221, 224, 229
Consumer Report, on marital therapy 182
contract rights 130
control 67, 97, 167, 197
conversation 35, 36–37, 150–51. *See also* intimate conversation
Corbett, William R. 117–19, 126, 136
crime 13, 173, 195
criminal conversation 115–16, 117–19, 126
cruelty, as grounds for divorce 179–80, 188
cultural influences 70
culture, on marriage 70, 91–93, 145, 162

deceit 240
Defense of Marriage Act 219–20, 224, 225
demands 39, 54–55, 81, 83, 85
democracy 223
Democracy Strategy 80
depression 172–73, 225

desire. *See* intimate emotional needs
deviant behavior 173
Dictator Strategy 78–79,
80, 83, 84
dictators 82
discrimination, against gays
and lesbians 9
dishonesty 53, 61–63, 98
disillusionment 100–1
disrespect 81, 83, 85
disrespectful judgments 39,
53, 56–58, 97
divorce 8, 13, 14, 16–17,
22–23, 95, 154, 156,
162
chaos of 170
consequences of 168–74
culture of 70–71
and financial problems
193
and health 172
incentives 192–94
and infidelity 113
and poverty 232
divorce laws 175–89,
210–11, 241. *See under*
Minnesota
divorce rates 92–93, 96,
104, 169, 189
of same-sex couples
215–16
domestic abuse 58–59, 173
domestic support 35, 48
dual careers 95–96
Dueling Dictators Strategy
79–80

economics, of marriage 10,
171–72
education 13, 171, 193
efficiency 46
emotional barriers 97
emotional disorders 172
emotional distance 152
emotional needs. *See* intimate emotional needs
emotional trauma 134
emotions 26
empathy 52, 64, 66, 76
engagement 123–24
enslavement, in marriage
102

enthusiastic agreement
75–76, 80–90, 223
exclusivity, of sexual services 128–29
extortion 124–27
extraordinary care 15,
24–25, 29, 32, 51, 58,
93, 105, 157–58, 159,
169, 238
and affection 40
and anti-buyer culture
199–205
cultural bias against 210,
218
and emotional needs
34–35
and interdependent
behavior 73–74
as mutual care 86
and permanence of
marriage 191, 204–5
restoring 239–41
extraordinary harm 61

failed marriages, stages of
100–1
family commitment 35, 48
family court system 184,
185, 187, 235
family law 121
father, influence of 214
fault 183
feelings 76, 78, 82, 83
feminists 93, 99, 101, 102,
118, 187, 194
financial problems, and
divorce 193
financial support 35, 48
forgiveness 157
Foster, Henry 187
free speech 138–39
freeloaders 196–205
frivolous lawsuits 117, 127

Gallagher, Maggie 241
gay and lesbian marriages.
See same-sex marriages
gay (word) 226
golden rule, in marriage
35–36
government assistance
192–94

Governor's Commission on
the Family (California)
180–85
Graber, Benjamin 45
grocery store exercise 89
grounds, for divorce 178
Grunsky, Donald 184
Gurian, Michael 99–102,
146, 195

happiness 32–33, 52
harassment 117
Hayes, James 184
health, and divorce 172
"heart balm" laws 134
homophobia 217
homosexuality, as mental
illness 225
honesty 35, 48, 63, 149

Idaho Supreme Court
127–28, 130, 137
important emotional needs
51, 96, 238. *See also*
intimate emotional
needs
incompatibility 85, 179
independence 53, 66–68,
72–73, 77, 102–3, 167
Indiana legislature 122–25
individualism 77
infidelity 14, 15–16, 103,
110–20, 218
discovery of 132
laws against 114–20,
122–25, 130–31
legalization of 115–16,
175, 210–11
suffering from 116, 134,
140–41, 144
Institute for American Values 169–70
Institute for Marriage and
Public Policy 241
intentional interference
with marriage 118–19
interdependence 73–74, 75,
103, 166, 167
Internet 131, 135, 138–39,
146, 162, 221, 234
intimate conversation
36–37, 43, 46, 147–48,
157, 162, 166

intimate emotional needs
36–45, 47, 49, 95, 146,
158, 159, 202
intimidation 117
"irreconcilable differences"
185, 237–38
"irretrievable breakdown"
182, 188

Jacob, Herbert 188

Kane, Frederick 123
Kay, Herma Hill 186–88
Kline-Graber, Georgia 45

laws
against infidelity 114–20,
122–25, 130–31, 235
encouraging infidelity
145, 238
marriage-unfriendly
231–34
and values 234
See also divorce laws
leisure 148
lies 62–63
lifestyle decisions 71
loss of love and affection
134
love 21–23, 34, 46–49
Love Bank 25–28, 32–33,
53–54, 147, 150
deposits 34, 68, 71, 72,
74, 88, 96
withdrawals 65, 68, 71,
72, 73, 77
Love Busters 52–68, 73,
98, 104, 158, 159, 240

mannerisms 64
"marital breakdown" 180,
182, 188
marital therapy. *See* marriage counselors
marriage
and child-raising 232
definition of 11–12

distortion of meaning
226
efficiency of 171
goal of 12–13
as obsolete 193–94, 209,
232
permanence in 100, 191,
235–38, 240
as safe environment 194
Marriage Builders Counseling Center 144
marriage contract 174,
176, 236–37
marriage counselors 97,
138–39, 162, 182, 232
marriage of convenience 79
Marriage Protection
Amendment 224
Massachusetts Supreme
Court 10
meeting other's needs
94, 95
men and women, profound
differences 99
mental illness 172
Minnesota
divorce law 115, 117,
123, 139–40
traditional marriage
amendment 7–8, 219–
20, 222, 224, 229
mistakes 39
mother, influence of 214
murder 154
mutual agreement 85,
87–88
mutual benefit 90
mutual care 86
mutual fidelity 129
mutually enjoyable lifestyle
67, 69, 74, 86, 98,
158, 159

National Conference of
Commissioners on Uni-
form State Law 186–88
National Opinion Research
Center 111
negotiation, in marriage
81–90

neurophysiology 99
Nevada, divorce laws 178,
187, 188
New York, divorce laws
177–79
Nicholson, Roberta West
122–23, 129
"No Child Left Behind"
program 14
no-fault divorce 17, 174,
179–89, 194, 221,
235–38

offspring 12–13
Oklahoma, divorce laws
179
openness 35, 48

panic 154
Parejko, Judy 189
parents 170
bad choices by 121–22
as role models 214
partial cause verdicts 136
passion, in marriage
199–200
perjury 178
permanence
of marriage 14, 16–17,
191, 201, 202–5
of romance 196–98
phobia 217
physical abuse 58–59
physical attractiveness
35, 48
physical needs 33
Policy of Joint Agreement
74–90, 158, 159, 223
polygamy 9, 227–28
poverty 171, 193–95, 232
power struggle stage 100,
101
precautions 135, 145, 147–
49, 153, 156, 159–60
Prichard, Tom 7
pride 225
private investigators 132
promiscuity 9
property, distribution after
divorce 222
property rights 130
punishment 61

rape 113–14, 144, 173
Reagan, Michael 189–90
Reagan, Ronald 180, 183, 184, 189
reconciliation 157, 237–38
recreational companionship 35, 36, 37–39, 43, 148, 150–51, 162, 166
relapse, into infidelity 156
renters 197–205
respect 57, 84–85
restoration, of marriage 153–59
revenge 137–38
Rhode Island, divorce law 189
Rockefeller, Nelson 178
romance, romantic marriage 25–29, 46, 103–4
  leads to disillusionment 195
  permanence 195–96
  rebuilding 149–50
  as stage of marriage 100–1
Rush, Locke 100

sacrifice, in marriage 86
safety 9–10, 12, 170, 216
Sally Jesse Raphael Show 133
same-sex couples, discrimination against 225, 227
same-sex marriage 9–10, 17, 209–13, 218, 225
  danger and fragility of 215, 225, 228
  as social experiment 217
scheduling problems 95–96
security 12, 170, 171–72
seduction 115–16, 117–19, 131
self-centeredness 16, 22, 70, 98
self-esteem 98
self-help books 22
self-sufficiency 167
selfish demands 22, 33, 53, 54–56, 78, 81, 97
separation 162, 179

sexual abuse 114, 144
sexual acts. *See* criminal conversation
sexual behavior, restrictions on 131–34
sexual exclusivity 14, 15–16, 138, 161, 234, 239–40
sexual fulfillment 35, 36, 43–45, 146, 148, 150–51, 160, 162, 166, 240
sexual harassment 119
sexual orientation 225
  changing 212–13, 226
sexual promiscuity 160–61
sexual services 128–29
sexually contracted diseases 226
Silent Revolution (Jacob) 188
South Dakota, divorce law 188
split shifts 96
spouse, death of 166
stability 216
  of marriage 9–10
state constitutions 210, 220–23, 224
suffering, from infidelity 116, 134, 140–41, 144
suicide 154, 172, 212
"superseding cause" argument 136
suppression, of instincts 159–60
Sweden, study of same-sex marriage 215–16

talk-show radio 221
Texas, divorce laws 179
thoughtfulness 55, 67
thoughtlessness 52–53, 67, 77
traditional marriage 231
travel 152
trust 62

understanding 38
undivided attention 38–39, 47–48
unhappiness 52, 53, 60
unhappy marriage 168–69
Uniform Marriage and Divorce Act 186–88
unilateral decisions 78–79, 82
United States Supreme Court 224
unmarried childbearing 232–33, 241

values 234
verbal abuse 59
Vermont, divorce law 188–89
victims, of infidelity 123, 143–44
violence 58–59, 173, 225, 236
vocational decisions 96
vows. *See* wedding vows

wants. *See* intimate emotional needs
wedding vows 11, 12, 15, 17, 22, 200, 239
welfare, and divorce 192–94, 232–33
Western civilization 227
white lies 62
win-lose solutions 86
win-win solutions 85, 86, 89
withdrawal, emotional 155–56
women
  as property of husbands 127–30
  trapped in marriages 92–93
  as victims of affairs 118, 123
working single mothers 194

zero tolerance policy (angry outbursts) 60

Willard F. Harley Jr., Ph.D., is a clinical psychologist and marriage counselor. Over the past thirty-five years he has helped thousands of couples overcome marital conflict and restore their love for each other. His innovative counseling methods are described in the books and articles he writes. Dr. Harley also leads training workshops for couples and marriage counselors and has appeared on thousands of radio and television programs.

Willard Harley and Joyce, his wife of forty-two years, live in White Bear Lake, Minnesota. They are parents of two married children who are also marriage counselors.

Be sure to visit Dr. Harley's website at www.marriage builders.com.

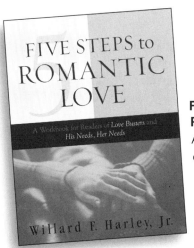

MORE BOOKS FROM

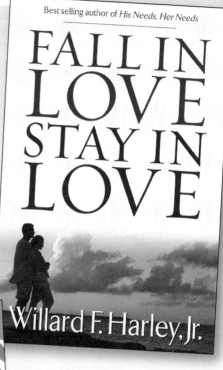

Fall in Love, Stay in Love
Dr. Harley's comprehensive program offers you proven steps for building a marriage that lasts a lifetime.

Best-selling author of *His Needs, Her Needs*

FALL IN LOVE STAY IN LOVE

Willard F. Harley, Jr.

mom's NEEDS

keeping romance alive
even after the kids arrive

dad's NEEDS

Willard F. Harley, Jr.
Best-selling author of *His Needs, Her Needs*

Mom's Needs, Dad's Needs
Dr. Harley shows you how to sustain a vibrant marriage during the childrearing years.

DR. WILLARD F. HARLEY, JR.

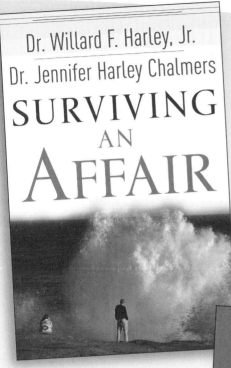

MARRIAGE BUILDERS

Building Marriages To Last A Lifetime

Dr. Harley has saved thousands of marriages from the pain of unresolved conflict and the disaster of divorce. His successful approach to building marriages can help you too.

Why do people fall in love? Why do they fall out of love? What do they want most in marriage? What drives them out of marriage? How can a bad marriage become a great marriage? Dr. Harley's basic concepts address these and other important aspects of marriage building.

At **www.marriagebuilders.com** Dr. Harley introduces visitors to some of the best ways to overcome marital conflicts and some of the quickest ways to restore love. From the pages of "Basic Concepts" and articles by Dr. Harley to the archives for his weekly Q&A columns and information about upcoming seminars, this site is packed with useful material.

Let Marriage Builders[TM] *help you build a marriage to last a lifetime!*
www.marriagebuilders.com